M000307734

Eerie Elegance

by
Britta Peterson

Britta Blvd Publishing

Eerie Elegance is an original publication of Britta Blvd Publishing.

Britta Blvd Publishing
2532 Rose Way
Santa Clara, California 95051 USA
publishing@britta.com

All text, photographs and illustrations copyright © 2008 by Britta M. Peterson
Published by arrangement with the author
ISBN: 978-0-9815871-0-3
www.EerieElegance.com

All rights reserved, which includes the right to reproduce this book or portions thereof in any form whatsoever except as provided by U.S. Copyright Law.
For information address Britta Blvd Publishing.

First edition: August 2008

Printed in the U.S.A.

Enormous thanks to...

My editing and development crew, whether early on or in the final crunch:
Natasha, Tracia, Nathania, Teje, Robin, and my mom Diane.

All my fellow Halloween fans from all over the globe.
It is always so much fun to hear from you!

All my party guests, friends & family over the years for being my captive audience!
I hope you've had as much fun as I've had!

Everyone's encouragement and support over the years caused me to write this book,
so I couldn't have done it without you all!

I hope you enjoy Eerie Elegance!

Table of Contents

An Introduction to Eerie Elegance

This book has developed out of my experience of hosting over a decade of Halloween parties that have since expanded into other theme parties throughout the year. For over ten years I have hosted a website documenting my Halloween parties and recipes with detailed pictures. My parties have become more elaborate over time, starting just out of college on a very restricted budget, then compounding on my prop collection and growing budget to enhance the experience each year. Nowadays, these are "parties as performance art" as elaborate as my budget and time will allow, since they are such a fun chance for me to express my artistic side. I try to have something new for each party. I find it fun to brainstorm and bring my ideas to life, and I have an instant audience in my party guests. Personally, rather than extreme gore or horror, I prefer my spooky-ookiness with a twist of classic style, causing friends to describe me as "a mix between Martha Stewart and Tim Burton," hence "Eerie Elegance."

I understand that some of my "extreme" Eerie Elegance might be intimidating for some to try and duplicate for themselves, but there are simpler variations that can be done by anyone, and some of the ideas are much easier to do than you might think. I have arranged each section to describe the simplest setup first, then what enhancements you can add if you feel so inclined. Also remember that you can always start simple, then add more later, which is exactly what I have done over the years. Before you know it, you just might be the talk of your friends for your own parties!

How to Host a Haunt

First, I have some basic party hosting advice for all your parties no matter how simple or extravagant. I have hosted many elaborate parties over the years, Halloween and otherwise. Often I plan months in advance and have detailed to-do lists, but even for smaller parties I am still always working down to the wire to get everything ready for guests to arrive! Needless to say, whether large or small, organization is the key to a successful elaborate party.

Plan ahead! Lists are your friends!

Do as much as you can in advance of your party. Plan out a schedule of what tasks can be completed early, like putting up decorations, organizing party favors or prizes, making quiz sheets, and what must be done closer to party time, like the food. Many cookies and appetizers can be made ahead and either frozen for reheating, or kept in airtight containers up to a week. A sample to-do list for my annual Halloween party is included at the end of this book. Write out your schedule for each day, especially the last week before the party, to be sure you don't forget anything, but also be sure you don't try to squeeze more than 24 hours into each day!

Brainstorm and save your ideas

Jot down all your brainstorms of what you would like to do for the party, whether for decorations, food, games or other activities. Write everything down even though you will probably have more ideas than you could possibly ever accomplish for one party. Once you have everything written down, go back and choose what is really feasible for you based on your time, budget and crafting comfort level. Remember if you start with good basics with just a few quality decorations and props that will last, you can save those to use again. Then you can spend your planning time in future years on new enhancements. When you have many of the same party guests each year, they will enjoy something new each party. For your own creativity's sake, you will also want to do at least something new each time, too. Who wants to do the exact same thing every year? If there are ideas you cannot do this year, save them to remember for next year or later. I have some ideas from several years ago that are still on my list to be included in future parties.

Create your party atmosphere

Your party decorations can be as simple as a food table with a few fun accessories, as elaborate as stone castle walls with a starry sky ceiling in your living room, or anywhere in between. Even small touches like candles and flowers can add that special something to your party atmosphere. Later chapters have decoration ideas for any size budget to help you create your party mood.

Do not limit yourself to purchasing during the party season

Hardcore Halloween fanatics already know this, but keep your eyes open for opportunities year-round. A trip to a thriftstore at any time of year might turn up tarnished silver candelabra perfect for your castle table or some interesting glassware for a mad scientist lab or potions study. Post-Christmas clearance sales could provide lightweight angels for possible gravestone decorations. Of course, post-Halloween sales will provide quite a few eerie items to add to your collection as well. Even your dry goods for your party recipes can be purchased well in advance when they are on sale instead of immediately before the party. Dry gelatin packets last almost forever if kept away from moisture. Canned juices and plastic bottles of soda also last a long time, but check the expiration dates so you don't keep them too long. Many ingredients are also freezable, so as long as you have the freezer space, get those when they are on sale as well.

Many hands make light work

Yes, it is a well-worn saying, but it is true! I have done countless parties all by myself, but it has always gone much more smoothly with assistance, especially from good friends. The only trick is knowing your helpers and what they feel comfortable doing. If they are willing helpers but not as comfortable with intricate decorating tasks, what about arranging cookies, lighting candles, mixing up punch, or even last-minute cleaning? There is always something on my list that can use the help!

Know your guests and plan activities accordingly

Different groups of guests will want to do different things at your parties. At an all-adult party your guests might just want to eat, drink and chat, with maybe a costume contest and a quick quiz or two. Too many planned activities might seem too juvenile for an adult party, but if your guests are young at heart, they may ask for more quizzes, especially when competition for prizes is involved! A party for all small children should have programmed activities so they are occupied and not becoming mischievous out of boredom. If you have a range of ages, try to have at least one or two activities targeted to the age groups, but hopefully some where all can participate together as well.

Last, but not least, have fun!

Of course you want everything to be perfect for your guests and exactly how you envisioned, but no matter how well you plan, something unexpected will always happen. Your fog machine may run dry and ruin the pump, your webcam might stop working, voting ballots could go missing, you might run out of punch, you may be late getting your own costume on while guests are already arriving...but remember it is a PARTY which is supposed to be fun! Your guests will be forgiving of any small glitches, and they might be so impressed with everything else you have done that they might not even notice anything *you* think is missing. Be sure to have fun at your own party, too!

Frugal Festivities

Clustering a variety of basic candles together brings wonderful Halloween atmosphere to your party.

When I started hosting my parties, I didn't have much money, and I still do search for the best deal for my hard-earned money, but I am able to splurge on more these days. The elaborate parties I have had in recent years are possible not only because I have more money to spend and I consider my party budget part of my personal entertainment budget, but also because I have the basics I've saved from year to year, so I can just keeping adding to them.

For instance, I have been using the same huge black plastic cauldron for over 8 years now. I sanded the outside surface so it looks more like cast iron, but it was one of the cheap

cauldrons you see everywhere around Halloween. I have also found maybe one or two more candlesticks each year, so now I have quite an extensive collection that I can also use throughout the year for other parties and holidays. So, what can give you the most pow for your party purchases?

Creepy Candlelight

You can get cheap candles at discount stores or on sale, and lots of candles, if used safely, especially without other lamps or bright light sources, always helps set the Halloween mood. Thriftstores are excellent sources for inexpensive props, including nice candlesticks, potions glassware and even some silver trays. Of course jack o'lanterns are the most common Halloween candleholder, but you can also use gourds, apples and miniature pumpkins to hold taper candles or tealights. Be sure never to leave burning candles unattended, do not let them burn all the way down to nothing, and keep them at least 12 inches away from walls or furniture. Keep lighted candles out of high-traffic areas and out of the reaching pathways on food tables.

In the past few years, battery-powered candles have become popular and very cheap at discount stores, however, they do not flicker and they do not give off as much light as each real flame candle. LED "flicker" candles are also becoming popular, but they are still not as bright as real candles. You might want to mix real candles with battery candles to add to the illusion. Still, battery-powered candles in wall sconces and on party tables are an excellent solution for high-traffic areas or around children where open flames might be dangerous. Also, in warmer weather, battery candles don't give off the heat that open flames do, so your guests are more comfortable. In the decorations chapter, I have a tip for turning the plain white battery-powered candles into more realistic colored candles.

Inexpensive Atmosphere

Even with your candles flickering and the lights turned off, you might want the room darker yet for a spookier mood. I used cheap black paper tablecloths stapled to the walls and ceilings for several years, but even though that idea is cheap and disposable, it takes a long time to put up and take down, especially getting the staples out, and the tablecloths don't last through the undecorating process to save them for later use. It is also extremely dark since everything is flat black, which just soaks up all the light

in the room. I have found fallen tree branches for free and propped those up in corners of the room for an outdoor atmosphere. Willow branches are great because the leaves are nice and long. I also made candle branch sconces out of shrub branches pruned from my parents' yard with recycled glass jars to hold tealights, so candlelight flickered through making large shadowy branch shadows on the walls. You can even use previous costumes as decorations with decorated foam wig stands for heads, like my witch who hovers over my cauldron, and

my friend with scissors for hands peeking over my china hutch. Look around to see what you might have for free for inspiration!

Potluck Parties & Prizes

Although you might like having control over the appearance of your spooky food, you can also cut down on the total party cost by having your guests bring drinks and food to share. You can even make the spookiest food a Creepy Cuisine contest with a prize and have everyone vote for their favorite. Many of the party activity ideas listed in this book can be done very inexpensively. As for prizes, all my prizes are cheap silly things that I get at discount stores or party stores. When these are wrapped up as a prize or chosen out of an overflowing treasure chest, even adults are always glad to win. How can you say no to an eyeball whoopee cushion?

Dastardly Decorations & Paranormal Paraphernalia

Mix and match projects from this chapter or use them as inspiration for your own designs to create your own spooky party atmosphere.

Transform Your Territory

I have always liked the concept of transforming my normal, everyday living space into a completely different space for Halloween. When your guests cross the threshold into a magical place they never expected, seeing them look around in wonder and hearing them ooh and ahh is such a great feeling!

Even small touches can go a long way toward enhancing your environment. For any decoration display, clustering your props together makes more of an impact. If you only have one or two props placed around a normal room, your guests might miss something really clever, but if you cluster those same few props in one place, you will have a theme that even if in a small area, will make more of an impact your guests will definitely notice. My gargoyle collection gets much more attention as Gargoyle Corner rather than sprinkled individually around my party. Even if you do have a lot of props, still tailor your decoration displays to the scale of the space you do have. You still have to have room for your guests to have fun!

Flagstone Walls

In my early Halloween party days I stapled disposable black paper tablecloths to my walls and ceiling. Cheap, but highly labor-intensive! I did get annoyed that the walls were too black and soaked up every last photon of light, which is why I tried one year with normal white walls, but even spookified with candles and decor it was much too bright for my vision of Halloween. I found black gossamer for really cheap in 2000, but even though it was a mottled effect instead of solid black, I also thought that was too dark overall. Since 2001 I have used the same flagstone-pattern gossamer and I love it! I was able to use the same roll of flagstone gossamer for 8 parties in two different places I lived, so not a bad investment for less than $200 for the 100 yards by 5' roll.

This material is actually non-woven fabric called "gossamer" that is available from party supply

stores online, sometimes in retail stores as well. If you search online for "flagstone gossamer" you will find all the online stores who sell it so you can compare prices including shipping costs. You can use normal paper to cover your walls, but paper can rip easily and is actually heavier to hang than the very thin gossamer. Also, paper will crease and is more difficult to roll up to save from year to year, whereas the gossamer rolls up fairly easily, and any creases can hang out over a couple days, or you can stretch the gossamer under tension at top and bottom to pull out any creases. The gossamer is slightly translucent, so the color of your walls will show through the pattern.

To hang the gossamer I use double-sided foam mounting tape on the top of the wall at the ceiling, using about 1-inch strip of tape every 8 inches or so, anchoring the gossamer as tightly as possible against the wall. The foam mounting tape is usually easy to peel off most surfaces, but sometime there can be some scraping involved. I have only had problems with paint peeling when the paint was a very thin layer over a glossy surface. The problem is that the largest the flagstone gossamer comes is 5 feet tall, so you will have a seam since most standard house walls are 8 feet tall. This means you will need to purchase

twice as much as your wall length, so measure and calculate carefully. I put my seam towards the bottom of the wall so it won't be at eye level for most people. Even pulled tightly across the wall, the gossamer can gap at the seam, so taping it holds it better, either clear cellophane tape or more mounting tape on the wall behind the gossamer seam. If you plan to use the same gossamer in the same place for future years, before you take it down, hand-sew it together at the seam with large basting stitches using matching gray thread. That takes awhile, but if you consider it an

investment for future years, you will be glad you did. I can definitely say that it is a lot of work to put the walls up the first time, and very tedious to hand-sew them together, but if you plan ahead, roll them up and label them well, putting them up the next time is much, much easier.

Tissue Paper Stained Glass Windows

You can make very inexpensive faux stained glass from corrugated cardboard frames with cheap colored tissue paper as the glass panes. Because tissue paper is so delicate and the dye will run, these are not suitable for anywhere moist, so only use these under cover or inside. First design your window on a large flat sheet of cardboard or foamcore board. For a diamond pane design, be sure to measure and use a straight edge. For

a freehand design, you can sketch first then widen the lines into a "leading" pattern that will be stable when cut. Cut your leading design out very carefully with a craft knife, since this is your structural integrity for your window to stay together. If you intend both sides to be seen, trace your cut board onto another sheet to cut a matching sheet for the back. Paint your board black with leftover paint, even tempura or spray paint. After the paint is dry, turn over and glue the cut panes of tissue paper to the unpainted side of the cardboard in the pattern of your design. I have made simple designs as well as elaborate pictures using this technique.

Fabric Stained Glass Windows

I had been getting frustrated that I could have all this wonderful dark atmosphere everywhere else, but since my kitchen light always had to stay on to keep getting food and drinks ready, the bright, fluorescent kitchen light showing from the pass-through to the rest

of the apartment spoiled the Halloween atmosphere I had carefully created in the other rooms. I had made cardboard and tissue paper stained glass windows before, but those are very fragile to store from year to year, so I thought fabric would roll up for easier storage. I did consider sewing it for the best stability especially when rolled up for storage, but since it was so large, I was

afraid that with pinning and sewing it, I might end up with puckers or it wouldn't hang as flat for sure. Instead, I carefully cut out two matching solid pieces of black felt by the yard with all the diamond-shaped holes. The matching black felt is to look good from both sides. Dress sheers like in the formal dress section of the fabric store are actually too sheer and don't show much color when lit from behind, since I tested by holding

fabric up to the light in the fabric store before I bought anything. I used cheap lining fabric in the jewel tones, cut out my diamonds out of various colors with a "seam allowance" to overlap the black felt "leading" pattern. With it laying flat on the floor on a sheet of cardboard to protect my carpet as well as keep everything as flat as possible, I then used fabric glue, so it would remain flexible to roll up for storage, and glued all the lining fabric diamonds between the two cut sheets of felt. I originally hung it from a tension rod in the pass-through in my apartment's kitchen, so I sewed a rod pocket at the top, with enough of an edge flap to reach the ceiling at the top above the rod pocket so no light would peek through. When I moved and instead of a pass-through I had the kitchen open to the dining area, I still used the fabric window to block off the kitchen light, but I had to add more felt to make a whole fake wall out of it. I used white felt for the wall portions and sewed some of the same flagstone gossamer I used for the rest of the walls so that it would complete the illusion. I could still get in and out of the kitchen since the window and "wall" to the floor became a flap door, which held shut by magnets.

Branch Candle Sconces

My branch candle scones started as inspiration from pruning scraps when my father was gardening. I chose the best branches that would work as sconces, then I found a recycled glass jar for each that would hold a votive candle. (Tip: the Tricky Crab Triangles recipe uses cheese that comes in the perfect glass jars for votive candles and tealights, so I always save them.) Note that

all the supplies are free so far, so this is a great project for a small budget! I hung the branch with fishing line monofilament on the wall after positioning the branch how it would stay stable against the wall, then I used epoxy glue to fix the glass jar where it would fit upright nicely in the branches, as much in the middle away from the wall as possible so the candle would make nice shadows on the wall behind. Hot glue gets too warm with the lit candle inside so the jar falls, which could be dangerous with a real flame. As long as your wall is a solid color and not too dark, when you light the candle inside the glass jar, you get wonderful spooky shadows from the dead branches. You could also use a battery-operated tealight in the jar, but the shadows will be more subtle since the light is not as bright as a live flame.

Spooky Spectres

For Halloween 1999, when I was experimenting with not making the decor quite so dark, I had the idea to create some spooky ethereal ghosts using loose-weave unbleached muslin, clear plastic latex gloves, and cheap plastic skulls. The effect is pretty good for such simple components. You can use any kind of fabric, even

old bedsheets or other scraps you may have, but the loose-weave muslin or cheesecloth flutters nicely and is just transparent enough to reveal the skull underneath the shroud. The plastic skulls usually are not painted very well, so I age them myself with brown acrylic paint, rubbing off the excess with a paper towel. These skulls are very thin lightweight plastic and hollow, so fishing line monofilament stapled to the ceiling is sufficient to hang the ghost. Thread some monofilament into the top of the skull, making a large loop tying the ends together, which is easier to hold a tight knot than a single thread with knots on each end. Thread the top of the loop with the knot through the middle of the loose-weave muslin piece, then anchor the knot to the ceiling using a staple gun or a cup hook. If you don't want arms, you can stop here for a very simple ghost. To continue with arms, inflate two latex gloves

and tie the ends just like balloons. Make more loops of monofilament, and arrange the loop around the palm of the inflated glove, then use the knot in the loop to thread through one edge of the muslin to drape as a sleeve. Anchor the knot at the ceiling in the same way as the head, and arrange the hand and sleeve to your liking. Repeat with the other glove to make and hang the other sleeve. Voila! A simple, cheap, spooky spectre! I have used these ghosts many years now, and for easy storage and setup, I keep the muslin over the skull with the monofilament threaded through the muslin, and the hand lines threaded too, so I only need to inflate new gloves for the hands. The latex gloves will start leaking air as they age, and they are cheap enough to use a new pair of gloves each year. These ghosts hang nicely from trees outside, especially coming alive when they flutter in a light breeze.

Battery Candle Sleeves

Battery-powered taper candles have become popular recently. I first saw them for several dollars each, but finally invested when I found them at a discount store two for a dollar! The cheap ones are just a normal incandescent bulb so does not flicker, but the main drawback for me is the plain white plastic shaft that ruins the illusion even more. From my extensive experience using hot glue guns, I figured I could make "wax" drips on a candle sleeve, then paint them any color I wanted for various holidays.

I already had some clear acetate scrapbook pages that would easily bend around the shaft and cut to size with any scissors. Once you cut the rectangle to size to fit     around the shaft with some overlap, wrap it around the shaft so it won't slide off but not so tight you cannot remove it. Use your glue gun to glue the entire seam completely, and run a "wax

 drip" bead the entire length of the seam to hold it shut. Continue making more wax drips around the entire top of the shaft where the bulb is, with the wax buildup edge higher than the edge of the candle shaft to hide the screw top where the bulb mounts. When the bulb is lit, the top of the candle glows just like a real candle does. Remove the sleeve from the candle, and use a thin tube or stick to hold the candle sleeve for spray painting the color of your choice. Normal spray paint will eventually flake off over time, but is usually  good for at least a few years. A satin finish gives the best candle look, since gloss is too shiny, but matte finish looks less like candle wax.

One drawback to the battery candles is they do not give out anywhere near as much light as real flames candle for candle. Mixing battery candles with real flames, like the example to the right, is a good compromise, especially if all real flames gets too warm or are unsafe in certain locations. Be aware of this when planning your party lighting, since if you use all battery candles only, your guests might not be able to see to appreciate the rest of your activities or decor!

 ## Peeping Portraits

The Blue Lady Portrait is a fantastic illusion for being so simple. I painted her with basic artist acrylics over an existing thriftstore framed canvas, then cut out her eyes since I wanted to find a motion sensor that would make her eyes move as people walked by, but I didn't get that finished. The next year, I just drew some eyes on paper that looked directly ahead and taped them behind the holes cut in the canvas. Lo and behold, just  recessing the eyes and having them look directly ahead makes them follow you around the room! Instead of painting your own portrait, you can buy a printed portrait from a poster store or print out images from online, cut out the eyes and replace them with ones that look directly ahead that are recessed from the rest of the portrait, and put your Peeping Portrait into a nice vintage-looking frame to hang in your own gallery or Haunted Hallway.

Haunted Hallway

At my apartment there was a short entry hallway that was perfect as a small area to decorate to make an immediate impact when guests entered through the front door. I tried several different schemes, including black light with fluorescent eyes on the walls with the branch sconces, but my favorite variation was my Haunted Hallway, loosely inspired by the Haunted Mansion and countless Scooby-Doo episodes. I found discount wallpaper for $2 per roll with a striped pattern and paisley pattern that matched well, plus a wallpaper border that looked like realistic dark wood crown molding. My mother had upgraded her lace curtains, so I had her previous lace curtains for free, then I bought cheap polyester blue crushed velvet for the other curtains. All the curtains were hung on tension rods across the hallway, and the wallpaper was only taped to the walls. I cut away a smaller portion of the crown molding border to make the chair rail and used the leftover strip as baseboard. The ornate gold and crystal candelabra was on sale at an antique store, and I already had the cheap small fern stand and the cheap oriental-style accent rug. My guests were expecting a plain white-wall apartment, but when they opened the front door they were quite surprised!

Trompe l'Oeil Pipe Organ

I have loved pipe organs for years even though I never learned to play one properly. Someday when I can finally build my own small castle, I want a chamber pipe organ inside it! Since I had success drawing with large sidewalk chalk on large black butcher paper for movie promotions, which requires very inexpensive supplies, I decided to try drawing some wall decor on black paper with chalk, including a pipe organ inspired by the library organ I had seen in person inside Blenheim Palace, Great Britain, with the angels of the original replaced by menacing gargoyles of course. The cheap black butcher paper only came 3 feet wide, so I carefully taped two 7-foot strips together lengthwise on the back side, then turned over the whole piece and drew with blue sidewalk chalk on the paper on a flat and smooth cement garage floor. Texture in your floor surface will show in the chalk design so be careful where you draw. I made the design so that my electronic keyboard with preloaded pipe organ sounds would fit in front to be the actual playable

organ. The original drawing stayed flat paper for several years, which conveniently rolled up for storage, but you must roll carefully and not let the final roll bend or get squashed, or the chalk can rub off and smear your design.

After seeing so many beautiful pipe organs and hearing them played so well while visiting Europe, I was inspired to enhance my pipe organ a few years later and make it 3D using foam sheets like I used to make my gravestones and outer stone walls. I cut the paper into 3 sections of the forced perspective and mounted them to the foam trimmed to match. The final foam pieces just leaned against the wall, then other foam pieces painted black surrounded the keyboard stand. This worked okay, and was perfect for my guest who came as the Phantom of the Opera, but I wasn't as pleased with the final result because of the mixture of flat vs. real 3D. On my future prop list is making a real 3D pipe organ, using leftover PVC pipe from my old back sprinkler system and an old electric organ found for free on the street, but that will have to wait until a future Halloween.

Tattered Curtains

The same inexpensive loose-weave muslin used for the Spooky Spectres can be used for old tattered lace curtains and much cheaper than the pre-distressed ones I have seen for sale in Halloween stores. Cut the lengths of fabric to size for your window, but don't worry about cutting neatly, since shredding the fabric and ripping by hand will give the most tattered look. You can take down your normal drapes and hang the tattered curtains in their place using clip rings or sewing a rod pocket, or you can drape the tattered ones right over your existing curtains. If your setting is the scene of a murder, maybe add some bloody handprints with red paint, like the victim was hanging on to the curtains for dear life.

Spiderwebs

It's just not Halloween without spiderwebs in some shape or form. The cheapest are the stretchable polyester webs all over stores around Halloween, but you must stretch them to their limit before they look right. Those webs take a long time to look good, plus are flammable, so beware of putting them near any real flame candles. I don't often use them myself, but I have seen them put to excellent use by others. However I do have spiderweb lace pillows and table runner, web wind chimes for outside, plus I have made a giant 8-foot diameter black rope web to hang on the ceiling. You can now find similar large rope webs at Halloween stores. Lately I have also been making a spiderweb design pastry brie, so spiders are well represented at my parties.

Mad Scientist Experiments
& Wizard Potions

Your Halloween display can easily include a mad scientist's laboratory or an alchemist's or wizard's study. These are very similar displays and can be customized by the accessories you choose. You can have a simple display just by arranging bottles and jars, you can make it glow from beneath using black light on a plastic or glass stand, or you can use these as fun "mix-your-own-drink" stations for party beverages!

Basic Mad Scientist Laboratory or Wizard Potions

The simplest mad scientist or potions display is just to find scientific or magical-looking bottles and jars from what you have, what you can find in various stores, and when you buy your groceries. Clean all those bottles well, removing labels where necessary. Cluster the glassware in an interesting assortment, adding colored liquids and your favorite accessories. You can start small and basic, then each year change one or two bottles or a few accessories for new ones you find over time. Before you know it, you will have quite a large and interesting glassware collection.

Bubbling and Smoking Potions

For any of the displays, you can add dry ice to make the liquids bubble and "smoke." It is safer to use dry ice in viewing-only displays rather than interactive displays. Remember to be very careful with the dry ice, since it will burn you if you touch it with your bare skin. I use a thick latex dishwashing glove, but even with that, you can only hold the ice a short time before the cold starts seeping through the glove. See the end of this chapter for more advice about using dry

ice. Since you purchase the dry ice in large slabs, I use a thick wooden cutting board underneath the ice with a small hammer and icepick to break up the dry ice slabs into small enough chunks to fit in the glassware. You want the smallest chunks you can get, because the more surface area that is on the ice chunk, the more bubbling you will have. The dry ice eventually cools the water around it enough so that there is no more sublimation ("smoke"), so a large chunk will bubble for awhile, then get a crust of normal water ice around it and the bubbling stops. It also helps to have the warmest liquids you can to get the most intense bubbling action. With warm water and lots of small dry ice chunks, you can even hear it bubbling!

What to Use for Scientific Glassware

When I started my mad scientist displays, I only had two small volumetric flasks that were extras from university chemistry lab classes. The rest of the glassware for my first mad scientist displays was just various vases and jars I had on hand. Plain, clear flower vases look enough like flasks for the effect, which is very convenient since most people have a few of those already. However, since I go to extremes and had always wanted more real scientific glassware in my display, in 2001 I bought a starter set of Erlenmeyer flasks and a starter set of beakers from an online laboratory supply store, so now I have real lab glassware. You can also find old scientific equipment and old apothecary bottles in thriftstores.

Mad Scientist Accessories

To find mad scientist accessories, brainstorm while looking around your house. You never know what you might have hidden in a closet somewhere! You can even print out scientific charts like the periodic table of the elements. Use a classic white lab coat hanging from a hook or draped over a chair, like the scientist has just stepped away. What else would a mad scientist have in his lab? Perhaps a lab report book for notes, preferably with detailed notes and drawings of experiments? Perhaps a (plastic) human skull for studying, dripping candles, or a stack of old spooky books? Maybe an old microscope? Any old electronics that look scientific, like an old oscilloscope? Perhaps even specimen jars of unrecognizable eerie things floating in colored goo?

Some easy accessories for specimen jars are the "grow-in-water" body parts popular around Halloween, like eyeballs, brains, hands, or ears. Those take several days to grow to their full size, so fill up your jar with water, including food coloring or non-toxic fluorescent paints if you are making a glowing display as described below, then add the shrunken body parts. Within a few days you'll have full-size body parts in the jar. One warning is not to use too much fluorescent paint (See "Glowing Mad Scientist Display") in the jars or the paint will settle onto the body parts instead of staying in the liquid. These will not glow as much because the body parts are in the way of the black light passing through the fluorescent liquid, so put them around the edges of a glowing display, letting the glassware glow brightly in the middle. After Halloween is over, you can drain the water and let the body part dry out again to save it for next year. It will take over a week to shrink back to the original size as the water evaporates completely.

Wizard or Alchemist Potions

Ideas for a mad scientist display can easily be adapted for an old alchemist's or wizard's potions laboratory. The only real differences are the types of glassware and the acces-sories. Keep your eyes open for interesting magical or old-fashioned-looking bottles when you buy your groceries, drink the contents, then wash them completely, remove all the labels, then add corks instead of screw tops for a more authentic look. Many craft stores are selling empty decorative bottles that look quite magical. Stacks of old books, lots

of candles, skulls, cauldrons, gargoyles, mummies, quills and parchment can all accessorize a wizard's study, even perching a pointed hat on a chair, as if he has only stepped away from his research for a moment.

Glowing Mad Scientist Display

Glowing liquids in beakers and flasks give the spookiest effect for these displays, especially if the potions are bubbling and smoking. Even though non-toxic paint is used so it should not hurt anyone, this "classic" version is for display only and not intended to be ingested.

You will need

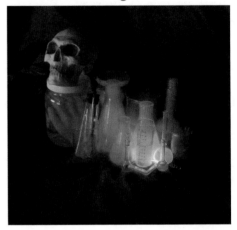

non-toxic fluorescent poster paints
drinking straws
assorted beakers, flasks, apothecary jars, flower vases
(any glass or plastic containers that look scientific)
glass tabletop
black light fixture
opaque black tablecloth (disposable is best)
other scientific accessories (optional)

The basics of this display are that you use the fluorescent poster paints in a very dilute mixture with water and light them from below with the black light, adding dry ice as the final touch for bubbles and smoke. Too much paint in the mixture will not glow since it will no longer be transparent. Hiding the black light fixture from view is essential to keep the illusion. I found that drinking straws were cheap and easy tools to take a small amount of paint from the small containers, holding the suction with a finger over the top of the straw, then adding and stirring into the water, either directly in the decorative "scientific" containers, or into temporary mixing jars to later pour into your display. Jars or bottles with screw-top lids are convenient to shake to be sure the paint is mixed well. You can have fun mixing colors together. My personal favorites are glowing lavender and teal. Depending on what you have for furniture and your party setup, you can use any of these methods below for your setting or come up with your own twist.

Under the Counter

If you have a raised counter, you can arrange the bottle display on the counter and set the black light under the counter edge below. This does not hide the black light as well as other methods, but it is the most basic setup. The black light does not have a very long range, especially with other light sources in the room, so it must be as close to your display as possible while remaining hidden. Arrange your glassware in a line along the length of the black light, as close to the edge of the counter as safely possible, and hiding the black light fixture as well as you can.

Glass Tabletop

A low glass coffee table is perfect for this display. Set the black light under the coffee table, then use a cheap black paper or vinyl tablecloth and make sure it reaches all the way to the floor on all sides and covers the entire table. Arrange the flasks and jars the way you like, then mark where they sit on the tablecloth. Cut out the hole in the tablecloth where you have marked the display, but make sure the hole isn't larger than the outer edges of your cluster of glassware. If the hole is smaller than the edges of your glassware cluster, everything will still glow enough, but if the hole is too large, you will give away your black light source under the table since it will shine through. Using vinyl tablecloths is often more convenient since there is usually enough moisture to disintegrate a paper tablecloth so it cannot be saved for future use, but a vinyl tablecloth can be used from year to year.

Other Glass Tables

If you don't happen to have a glass or clear plastic table already, there are inexpensive round "designer" or "decorator" tables sold at discount home decorating stores with matching glass round tops. As long as you set the glass top up on supports, you can still fit the black light fixture underneath the glass, then follow the instructions above about cutting the hole in the tablecloth. In this case, since the light fixture is already blocked by the wooden top, you won't have to worry as much about the tablecloth reaching all the way to the floor.

Drinkable Experiments and Potions

If you use the same glassware and accessories but change what is inside the glassware, you can make a "mix-your-own-experiment" or "mix-your-own-potion" beverage station. The most basic method is just to find interesting bottles for your theme, put different colored juices and sodas in them, all safe to drink, then find fizzing candies, gummy worms, candies, dried fruit, and other interesting-looking ingredients, and let your guests have fun! Plain small disposable plastic tumblers are perfect as mixing beakers. Glowstick bracelets from craft stores and discount party stores, also available online, make fun stir sticks for these drinks.

Because I take everything to the next level, I elaborated on my display because I thought my guests might be allergic to an ingredient or just want to know what they really were, so I labeled every bottle. The labels include the "chemical" or "magical" ingredient on one side of the label, with the real ingredient on the back, then the labels are tied to the bottles. I researched what chemical compounds were what colors and textures, so I tried to match those with real ingredients that were similar but safe. If you feel comfortable serving alcohol because you are having an adult party, include liquors like black vodka, cream liqueurs and other colored liqueurs for variety, since the bar staples like vodka, rum and tequila are usually clear. I had fun naming my ingredients, since I thought the straight alcohols were like the strong chemical acids. "Aqua Fortis," literally "strong water," the old alchemy term for nitric acid, was perfect for vodka. You can also use carbonated sodas as your strong acids, especially with a sharp lemon-lime or citrus flavor to be acidic. If you want healthier drinks, use a variety of fruit juices and name them creatively. Of course small children will just enjoy mixing different bright colors together, and if they have icky names that are funny, all the better!

This drinkable potions idea is even more fun when combined with a contest. Have potion recipe cards on parchment paper or lab report papers on graph paper ready for your guests with instructions for them to create their own concoctions, writing down what it does (levitation? transformation? time travel?), the ingredients they used, and a clever title. When all their sheets are completed, have the entire party vote on their favorites, with a prize for the winner.

Here are some possible ingredients with their real counterparts, but don't let this stop you from creating your own!

Mad Scientist Experiment Ingredients

ectoplasm = loose set lemon gelatin dessert - nice and slimy!
phenolphthalein = pink grapefruit juice
"spirit of salt" hydrochloric acid = light rum or lemon-lime soda
perchloric acid = spiced rum, caramel syrup or cola
tincture of iodine = dark rum, chocolate syrup or root beer
spirit of vitriol = sulfuric acid = Bacardi 151 rum or ginger ale
benzene = peach schnapps or peach syrup
phosphoric acid = cranberry juice
"aqua fortis" nitric acid = vodka or tonic water
life blood extract = raspberry syrup
silicon dioxide = granulated sugar
sucralose = Splenda sweetener
sodium chloride = table salt
carbonic acid = diet tonic water
lactic acid compound = caramel cream liqueur, milk or cream
copper sulfate = blue sports drink
ethylene glycol = green sports drink
tincture of zinc = bright green Midori melon liqueur
citric acid = pineapple juice (there is citric acid in pineapple juice!)
Agent Orange = dark orange tropical juice drink
lithium carbonate = crimson flame = red fizzing candies
copper = blue flame = orange fizzing candies
zinc or copper acetate = green flame = green fizzing candies

eyes of newt = silver dragees
leech juice = cranberry juice
elderflower wine = green sports drink
nettle wine = blue sports drink
pamplemousse juice = pink grapefruit juice
pureed phoenix feathers = pineapple juice
fluxweed juice = purple grape juice
Aqua Fortis = vodka or tonic water
shredded snake skin = blue & black edible glitter
beetle eyes = black sugar crystals
dried bee stings = thin chocolate jimmies
powdered unicorn horn = powdered sugar
cut ginger root = cut ginger root
chopped daisy root = shredded coconut
sliced caterpillars = sliced dried mango
lacewing flies = clear edible glitter
dried nettles = thyme leaves
puffer fish eyes = white non-pareils
crushed snake fangs = granulated sugar
crushed scarab beetles = fine black sugar
rat tails = thin black string licorice
chopped tube worms = chopped gummy worms
porcupine quills = dried rosemary
dragon eggshells = white chocolate flakes
mint leaves = mint leaves

How to Handle Dry Ice Safely

Dry ice creates a wonderful and fairly cheap smoke effect, but there are safety concerns. Any reputable dry ice supplier should give you a safety pamphlet when selling you their dry ice, so pay attention to those instructions as well as these tips.

"Dry ice" is solid carbon dioxide (CO_2), which is the majority of what animals, including humans, exhale every time they breathe, so the carbon dioxide molecule itself is not toxic. The bubbles in any carbonated drink like your favorite soda are mostly carbon dioxide bubbles. However, to force carbon dioxide into solid form, it requires a much lower temperature than ice made from water. This means that the severe cold of dry ice can cause burns to unprotected skin, so please be EXTREMELY careful when handling dry ice and using it around food or beverages. The fun part about solid carbon dioxide is that at standard room temperatures and above, it skips the usual "melting" transition from solid to liquid before turning into vapor, so it goes directly from solid to vapor, called "sublimation," which is the fog or "smoke" you see. The warmer the temperature around the dry ice, the quicker the sublimation process, which is why warm water is often recommended to get the rolling bubbles you see so often in mad scientist displays or witches' cauldrons.

When dry ice is put into warm water, the sublimation process continues until the water is cooled below the sublimation point, which means solid water ice forms as a crust around the dry ice. Even adding more warm water to the container at this point does not trigger sublimation again until the crust of water ice is removed. The best technique around this problem is to use the smallest chunks of dry ice that you can (even little chips work for a minute or two), since then the dry ice all sublimates away before the water is cooled too much. This also requires more "babysitting" your display since the smaller chunks disappear into vapor more quickly as well.

Remember - you do NOT want anyone to eat or even touch any solid dry ice with any bare skin, let alone fingers, tongues or lips, since it can harm them. Then how have I used it in my punch cauldron safely? Well, I use a large 12-quart cauldron for my witches' brew, which is quite deep. Dry ice is heaviest so it will sit on the bottom, and my ladle doesn't reach all the way to the bottom of the cauldron without a lot of effort, so I was not that concerned. If you have carbonated soda in your punch, it's really cool when you get really big bubbles filled with the fog that pop at the surface, releasing a puff of "smoke" into the air.

I finally found a safe, reliable solution for putting dry ice into any size cauldron. A tea infuser ball is too small, since you would be refilling it every minute or so, however a large spice ball for mulled cider or wine has enough small holes to allow the fog to escape but not any physical chunks of dry ice. This is definitely worth the $8 I spent compared to my various prototypes made from hinging strainers together. Filling the spice ball with small chunks of dry ice lasted a good 15-20 minutes of vigorous bubbling, which is about as much time you get when dumping a bowlful of chunks directly into the cauldron. It comes with a chain to hang on the edge of the pot for easy retrieval, but in a punch bowl cauldron, you can always use the punch ladle instead if the chain falls in accidentally. I intend to use my spice ball for all cauldron dry ice effects from now on.

Many party stores will have seasonal Halloween sales of dry ice, but they usually charge more than if you look up "dry ice" in your local yellow pages. Some larger grocery store chains are now carrying a small bin of dry ice near the normal party ice bags. Bring an airtight ice chest with you to carry your dry ice home and help keep it as cold as possible until you want to use it. Do NOT put dry ice in your home freezer since the freezer can be permanently damaged! Try not to get your dry ice until the day of your party, or at least no earlier than the evening before your party if necessary. 50 pounds is usually enough to last through my party for my 12-quart cauldron of witches brew, my tabletop mad scientist display and a few other displays, plus some leftover the next day for my photo shoot of my decorations. I use a little hammer and an icepick on my wooden cutting board to smash smaller chunks from the large slabs, then use a plastic or freezer-safe ceramic bowl with gloves to scoop some chunks into the bowl then carry it to whatever liquid I'm using. By using the small chunks and leaving the rest in larger chunks together inside the ice chest still wrapped in their original paper wrappers, they help keep each other cold enough to last longer. You will need to keep adding more chunks of dry ice to your cauldron every 20-30 minutes or so to keep it bubbling really strongly, but gentler wisps of fog will keep going for longer. This "bubble maintenance" job to keep all the dry ice displays going while guests are till arriving is a good one to give to someone else while you continue preparing party food or re putting on your own costume. Once most guests have settled in, no longer paying as much ttention to the cauldron, "bubble maintenance" can take a break, returning later if you like.

After all these warnings please still be aware that you need to use your own judgment about using dry ice around food and especially in beverages. If your party is for kids or teenagers, I vould not put any dry ice in the actual punch at all, even inside a spice ball, nor would I if it was a rambunctious party with alcohol flowing so much people might not remember that solid dry ce can burn them. If your guests are reasonable adults and generally behave themselves, you night decide you can safely use dry ice in your witches' brew, too. Err on the side of caution if you are not sure of your guests. You know how your own party guests will behave better than could ever guess.

Haunted Headstones

I had Halloween parties with no graveyard and no headstones for many years, since I wanted to wait to make elaborate carved foam tombstones for my graveyard in a real yard outside, but I was always living in apartments upstairs. You might want to start with gravestones right now! How should you get started? That depends on how much time and effort you want to spend, your crafting confidence level, and what styles you like. Here are several choices for you, from the simplest display to the most elaborate fog-laden authentic-looking carved stone graveyard.

Purchased Headstones

Halloween has become a much more popular holiday in the past decade, so there are now many seasonal-only stores that sell very good quality props, but you pay for that quality. If you have the budget and you like their ready-made designs, you might as well buy the resin or elaborate foam gravestones sold by Halloween specialty stores since they will be an investment for years to come. You can find them locally starting in September each year, or you can search online and find all sorts of styles you can purchase year-round. Using this method you are not able to customize your designs or epitaphs.

Cardboard Headstones

Very simple and very cheap gravestones can be made from old cardboard boxes, gray paint, and a black or dark-gray felt-tip marker. Since they are only cardboard, they will not survive moisture, so these are best for inside or a controlled outside environment. This is a cheap craft idea for a children's Halloween party, and could be turned into a contest for fun-loving adults, with prizes for cleverest epitaph, best appearance or most creative.

You will need

cardboard boxes, various sizes, still intact (save from the recycling bin)
sharp craft knife or heavy-duty scissors
pencil or felt marker
flat gray paint, or white and black spray paint
black or dark-gray felt-tip marker

1. Set the box upright so the folded flaps are at the bottom, still glued together for stability.

2. Find the side you want to be the main gravestone face. Draw your design, but before cutting, on each side perpendicular to the front, draw a diagonal line from the back bottom up toward the front, as high as your front design will allow.

3. After all your lines are drawn, use a craft knife or scissors to cut out your basic shape. Your gravestone should stand on its own because you have the diagonal side braces still attached between the front gravestone face and the stable bottom.

4. Paint everything gray, either with "mistake paint" or flat finish spray paint which works fine and takes less time to dry. You can use a base coat of white spray paint, then a light dusting of black spray paint for a nice mottled stone affect, as pictured.

. Once the paint is dry, use the pen to write your epitaphs.
Dark gray will be more realistic as carving than plain black pen.
Pencil is good for sketching your design but usually too light
for the final detail. You can also use the pen to add some basic
carved-style designs to your gravestones.

Before painting you could embellish cardboard gravestones with
any small lightweight decorations, but if you are able to go to that much effort and expense for
party decorations, the construction foam is not that expensive, so you might as well make more
realistic gravestones that will last you longer using the foam technique.

Basic Foam Headstones

A step between cardboard gravestones and the fully-carved foam gravestones is to eliminate the
carving. In recent years, discount party stores and craft stores have been selling very basic gray
foam headstones with no decoration or perhaps just RIP at the top. This eliminates the step of
cutting the gravestone shapes. Otherwise, purchase thick foam insulation sheets from your local
home improvement store, cut out the outer shapes of the gravestones you like, then just paint
those basic shapes gray. If you have found ready-made embellishments you like, secure them
on the gravestones before painting with craft glue. Cool-melt hot glue can melt the foam so it
is safer to use craft glue and anchor in place while it dries. You can use lettering stencils with
dark gray paint, use a felt-tip pen to write the epitaphs and draw any "carved" designs, or even
try using a dull pencil or the end of a chopstick to "carve" lettering into the foam. Use a dark
gray pen instead of black for a more carved look. As long as you use a permanent marker, these
stones should be able to last through basic overnight moisture, but probably not any rainstorms
or automatic sprinkler systems. Store them carefully for the next Halloween, touching up any
chips in the foam with the gray paint, and you can use them year after year.

Ultimate Haunted Headstones

Now, the pièce de resistance! For Halloween 2003, I finally had a yard, so I was "dying" to make my own graveyard! Of course I needed gravestones, and I wanted to make my own. Since I have carved foam for stone looks before, I knew I would use insulation foam sheets, with some way to carve into them, but why reinvent the wheel when the World Wide Web is at your disposal? I searched online, since I had seen some basic instructions before, but I knew others had made more elaborate homemade gravestones, so I was hoping to take advantage of any tips they had. An online search and web-wandering from Halloween site to Halloween site led me to a fabulous site that is unfortunately no longer online. I have taken their original techniques and added my suggestions and clarifications of my own, especially because I could not find the blue "crispy" insulation foam sheets at any of my local hardware stores. The supplies listed below are easily found at larger-chain craft stores and home improvement stores.

First you need to design your gravestones. I visited a local cemetery with my camera and found some nice examples from the past 100 years, but on a visit to Great Britain I photographed many even older beautiful ones. You also need text for your gravestones. Depending on your personal taste, you might use humor like "Ida Voydre", or authenticity with gravestone rubbings or famous people's epitaphs, but for my first 13-stone graveyard, I used my favorite fictional characters and incorporated them into one of my party quizzes. I expanded my graveyard with six more stones the following year, still using the fictional character theme, but using the ones that were too obvious for the previous quiz.

Now that you have your inspiration designs, on to making your own Haunted Headstones!

Haunted Headstones Supplies

1-1/2 to 2-inch thick pellet-based foam insulation sheets (like "Insulfoam R-Tech")
pale-colored felt-tip pen or pencil
serrated kitchen knife (electric if possible saves hand fatigue!)
hot wire foam cutter (like "Wonder Cutter")
woodburning tool
garden hose
flat gray latex paint
black acrylic paint
flat black spray paint
medium-size old brush you don't mind mangling
fine point brush for enhancing carved detail
dimmer switch (optional)
lightweight embellishments like plastic or foam figures, clothesline or lines of beads (optional)

Carve and Decorate Your Stones

I use the "Insulfoam R-Tech" pellet-based foam insulation sheets from my local home improvement warehouse that come with the thin plastic film on each side of the foam. Two 4x8-foot sheets of 2-inch thick foam made 13 gravestones for me, including my double-sized House of Usher and my large black marble stone. The challenge was getting the full 4x8-foot sheets home!

Since the foam I found does not cut very smoothly, with the compressed pellets popping out still in pellets instead of cutting cleanly, I decided against using my power dremel tool for any engraving. Instead I purchased a cheap woodburning tool and used the smallest point in the kit. Be sure to remove the thin plastic film before cutting or engraving the pellet-based foam. If you have leftover foam you will save for future years, remove the film from the foam when it is still new, since the film can permanently adhere over time. Since the hot

wire foam cutter can only reach a couple inches into the foam sheet, you will need to rough-cut the shape of your gravestones first with a serrated kitchen knife. Don't worry, since the foam scraps easily clean off the knife. An electric knife makes this task even easier. After your gravestones are freed from each other, use the hot wire foam cutter carefully to create a smooth surface around all the edges of each gravestone.

Use a pale-colored felt tip pen or pencil to sketch the design onto your gravestone. If it helps, you can print out epitaphs from your computer in fonts that you like, then use carbon paper to trace them onto the foam. Even with the smallest tip, the woodburning tool is hot enough that it ablates the foam immediately, so the line you "carve" is about 1/4-inch wide, which doesn't allow for fonts that are too intricate. For my second set of

gravestones and onward, I added a dimmer switch to the woodburning tool, allowing me to control the heat at a lower level to make a finer point, which is perfect for intricate text designs. The fumes from the burning foam are indeed pretty foul smelling, so this is best done outside in open ventilation. I did use the largest tip that came in my set to recess the background around the lettering in some of my designs. I suggest that you practice using the woodburning tool on scrap foam first. You will notice that the longer you hold the woodburning tool in the same spot, the constant heat will keep eating away more and more foam, so be careful. You can also use that knowledge as a technique, realizing that going slower leaves a larger carved line, but going faster leaves a more delicate line. This is especially helpful for making cracks that start as a wide crack at the edge of the stone, but taper into hairline cracks in the main stone body.

You can embellish your gravestones with anything that is lightweight and paintable. It does not matter what color the embellishments are since the entire stone will be painted gray later anyway. For a more elaborate gravestone, you can build up layers of foam, as I did for Mina Murray's gravestone. Use clothesline or strings of plastic beads for decorative edging, and use figures to add sculptural texture to your stones. You can even make your own sculptural figures out of polymer craft clay baked in the oven, but remember that polymer clay figures larger than a couple inches might make a foam gravestone too top-heavy. I found perfect gilded plastic Christmas angels at a discount store, but since there were limited designs available and I was only making 13 gravestones at that time, I restrained myself to using one angel of each style. Use spray adhesive to glue together flat sections of foam, or strong white glue and patience for three-dimensional pieces, since remember even cool-melt hot glue is hot enough to melt your foam. All the rest of my decorations are just engraving with the woodburning tool, no extra molded pieces, but for Mina Murray's stone, I used a cheap night light of a veil-draped woman's head glued into a recessed area of the foam. I did try sanding flat areas to try a different surface effect, but sanding just starts making the foam pellets flake off whole. However, I do use the woodburning tool to engrave cracks and chips into my gravestones, which look quite effective.

Paint Your Stones

After all the detail work is finished and all glue is completely dry, it is time to paint. My flat gray latex paint was very inexpensive from the mistakes pile at my local home im-provement warehouse, so I definitely advise you to look there first. I only used about half the can for 13 gravestones. Make sure you completely cover everything with the gray paint first, since you will be using spray paint later that can melt your foam even through a tiny speck left unpainted. This is most difficult wherever you have carved, especially with small detail, so this base coat painting step takes the longest for me. Sloppily smash the brush loaded with paint into the carved sections, then move the brush around to evenly distribute the paint. I discovered that painting large flat areas in a random pattern and letting it stay splotchy gives an even better aged stone effect, so don't worry about getting the gray in an even coat, but do make sure you don't have stripes.

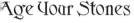

My one marble gravestone has a base coat of black gloss oil-based paint since I had a leftover can, then after the black was dry I used the standard faux-finish feather technique to make the white marbling pattern with white acrylic paint, paying attention to how the marbling would go around the edges and onto the back of the stone. I personally prefer the gray stone gravestones, so I stopped at only one marble stone. I also discovered that too much paint thinner in your oil-based paint can distort the surface of your foam, so try to find latex paint.

Age Your Stones

This black spray paint and garden hose technique is excellent, but it is a bit scary only at first. It helps if you think that you are just simulating hundreds of years of soot and dirt with your spray paint, and years of rain with the hose. If you think of it that way, you will get a more natural effect since you will use a very light "dusting" of paint each time. Be patient and do as many layers of spray paint

in one hand with the hose trigger in the other until you get the effect you like. It is easiest to prop the gravestone at about a 60-degree angle so the water runs off well but still pools per gravity, just like real dirt and rain would do over time. Don't forget to turn the stone to age the back as well. A rain-shower watering hose attachment works very well for this technique, since with the trigger allowing for different water pressure, you can control little rivulets of water where it needs more artistic assistance in the aging process.

Once the gravestones are completely dry from the garden hose and spray paint, the last step is to accent the carved detail by using watered-down black acrylic paint. This takes time but really does make a difference, as you can see in the photos. Real carved gravestones have lettering that is "blackened" to be legible, and when you see your gray aged stones, you'll understand why. If you use pure black paint too highly-concentrated, you will have too much contrast and your gravestone will no longer look realistic, since it will look drawn instead of carved. You can always add more thin layers of paint to build up to the correct shade, but you cannot easily lighten inside the detail if it gets too dark.

I have not sealed my gravestones, since I so far have been lucky with dry enough weather for my parties, and between parties they have been safely stored in my garage out of the elements. Hopefully some spray matte finish sealer will be fine, since you definitely do not want the stone effect shiny at all, but use at your own risk, since I am a bit scared if the sealer would ruin my beautiful gravestones that were so much work! Even when carefully stored from year to year, chips and cracks can happen, and glue can get old enough to loosen, so I have needed to touch up my gravestones, but they are holding up quite well. Accents can be re-glued, and an extra chip or crack just adds more character.

Display Your Stones

Of course you must first find an area for your graveyard. A flat lawn is often easiest to use, but beware of tricksters possibly vandalizing your painstaking work if you use your front yard. Arrange your stones the way you would like to display them, making sure that your clever epitaphs can be seen, but also resembling a graveyard. Offset your rows so the stones behind can be seen between the ones in front. Remember that real graves include the full length of the coffin between rows, but that often looks too open for a Halloween graveyard, especially if you only have a small space to decorate. By shrinking your scale leaving rows between but placing the headstones just 3 feet apart, it will still look enough like a graveyard without seeming empty.

To set up your graveyard, you have several choices of stakes, whether thin metal stakes, small bamboo gardening stakes, long roofing nails, or whatever else you find that fits your budget. You need your stakes to be thin to fit inside the thickness of your stone, but tall and strong enough to support your stone. This can be challenging with the larger and more elaborate gravestones. It can be easier for the largest ones just to lean artistically against a wall or tree or propped amongst landscaping as an overgrown graveyard. Be sure you make the holes carefully in the gravestones themselves, since the foam is not strong enough for you to push the entire gravestone with stakes into the ground. You don't want stakes poking through all your hard work! Be sure to make at least two holes in the bottom of your stone so it doesn't spin around on one stake in a breeze, then pound your stakes into the ground spaced appropriately for each stone. It is easiest to lay out your stones flat in your graveyard with the bottom edges in line where you want them, then go around with your stakes and pound them into the ground spaced the width of the holes in the bottom of each stone. If you are setting out your stakes well in advance of putting up the stones, use tape to make flags on the top of the stakes, or they can be hard to find later. Since you already have

your holes in the stones, you should be able to place each stone on the stakes in the ground. Voila, your very own graveyard! Piles of dead leaves, pumpkins and fog machines optional.

Graveyard Glow

My artificial moonlight is created with some clamp lights on extension cords, one at each end of the graveyard, so for the first year one was clamped in the tree by the gate where you entered the graveyard, then the other was in the taller tree at the opposite end. The hard part is placing them so the light doesn't stare into anyone's eyes but is still bright enough to see your graveyard. I do a test-run of the graveyard and the fog machines in the dark before my party, and hopefully the weather cooperates to leave the setup in place between the test run and the party. For only $40 at a discount store, I bought a portable lamppost for the next year, so I didn't worry about hiding that light source, but it was so bright it made it difficult to photograph. It was great for lighting though, and since I had two fog machines going, it looked fabulous with the light shining through the fog!

Ghoulish Games & Petrifying Pursuits

When people find my Halloween parties online, they often ask what party activities I plan. My parties these days are mostly mixing, mingling, drinking and eating, with a couple of games, too, but I find for adults it works best if you have fewer scheduled events to give people the freedom to chat, eat and drink. Here are some fun ideas you might want to include in your own parties.

Halloween Music

Of course no Halloween party would be complete without a spooky tune or two. Years ago I made two Halloween mix CDs of spooky songs to play in rotation at my parties, which are now digitized on playlists. Make sure the music is not so loud that your guests cannot hear each other easily.

Costume Contest

Halloween is the biggest costume event of the year, so a costume contest is an obvious choice. I always have my guests vote on costumes, and since it's often really hard to pick a real "Best Costume," I have expanded the categories to Most Original, Scariest, and Ultimate Costume so more people can win. You can just take a poll of hands, which I have done before, but since some people need to leave the party earlier than you want to tally the votes, I find it's easier to print out a little ballot. Print 4 to an 8.5x11" sheet of paper, then cut them after printing enough pages from your computer, then people who need to leave can still leave their votes behind for counting later.

Name That Spooky Tune

Since 1999 I have had a Name That Tune contest, always spooky themed, but even more specifically-themed in recent years to keep it interesting. You can find songs online for purchase and sometimes even for free download if you get lucky. Often party stores will sell inexpensive Halloween collections of music you can use. One year was spooky TV show themes with the Addams Family, the Munsters, Bewitched, Scooby Doo, Dark Shadows, Twilight Zone among others. Another year was spooky movie themes, including the Shining, the Omen, Ghostbusters, Nightmare on Elm Street, Scream, and more. My guests always seem to like that quiz, so it has become a tradition. I always have 13 tunes to name, of course!

Creepy Cuisine

Allow your guests to shine by bringing their own Creepy Cuisine to the party! Not only does this help you as host by offsetting some of the party food cost and effort, but also it gives your guests a chance to show off their own creativity. Running an actual contest for Best Chef might inspire your guests even more. I absolutely love how creative my guests can be! I have had to create extra prize categories on the spot because so many entries were so clever in their own ways. Be sure to have forms they can complete with the title and description of their dish so everyone can appreciate them, and don't forget to list their own name so you know who is the winner.

Other Quizzes

Some years when I have an idea I cannot resist, I have added an extra quiz that guests can do at their leisure instead of a scheduled event like listening to the music clips for Name That Tune. I have made up Spooky Scrambles, which was choosing classic spooky literature like Frankenstein, Dracula, The Picture of Dorian Gray, Dr. Jekyll & Mr. Hyde and others, and scrambling the authors' names so my guests had to unscramble them. The first year I made gravestones, I made the gravestone epitaphs a Haunted Headstones quiz, so my guests had to

closely inspect my hard work of creating the gravestones to identify the character, media, and creator of each character. Some were obvious and some were obscure, but they were all favorites of mine, and the highest score was 34 out of 39, so it was challenging enough but not so difficult to be discouraging. While researching epitaphs, I found many actual famous ones, so I have also made a Genuine Gravestones quiz to match the famous person to their actual epitaph. The original Spooky Scramble and Genuine Gravestone quizzes are provided in the back of this book for you to use at your own parties if you like. Be sure to make copies of the sheets without the answers!

Other Ghoulish Games

For a large party specific activities are harder to organize, but with less people, you can do other games. In past years we have done apple carving instead of pumpkin carving with voting on the designs we liked best. We have also done scavenger hunts, which are especially good if you are in an apartment complex so you can knock on doors close by to collect items from people. I have even done an "Easter egg hunt" with little pumpkins filled with candy instead of Easter eggs. There is also tag-team "Dreadful Doodles" where you have a list of spooky Halloween-themed words to draw, separate people into teams, then the doodler for each team comes to you to get the word then they go back & draw for their team to guess. As soon as the word is guessed by that team, their next doodler runs up to tell you the correct word they guessed, and to get the next word to draw. Since it's a race of who guesses your whole list of words first, it can get wild with people running back & forth, but it is pretty fun. You need a decent amount of space to be able to separate the teams, though. However, all those seem to be too much scheduled activity when you get a larger group of people who might just rather socialize, and my parties seem to keep getting larger and larger each year!

Saving Spooky Scenes

Y ou have worked hard on your Halloween party and decorations, and you are so proud that you would love to be able to show people who cannot be there in person. You took so many photos but they are either too dark or blurry, or too bright with flash. How come none of the photos you take capture the dark moodiness of your carefully-created Halloween atmosphere?

Documenting your Decor

Depending on your decor, no flash at all might be better to capture your setting, like the image to the right, but I have found that slow-sync flash is your friend! Not all cameras have that setting, or they might have something similar like "night mode" but not called a flash setting. Slow-sync flash means that it actually sets the exposure setting for no flash, leaving the shutter open awhile first to capture the ambient lighting, then it uses the flash right before closing the shutter to freeze the action. Of course, you can still have issues like camera shake or moving subjects when the shutter is open before the flash goes, so keep that in mind. That is why I use a tripod whenever possible, which gives good results for me. My tripod is very lightweight, but the legs have two segments that stretch out and the top can be raised almost to my eye level, which makes for more realistic photos, too, since they're shot at the same vertical level as most people would view the scene in person.

All the photos in this book were taken with consumer-level cameras, either digital or 35mm film. Using a tripod, paying attention to your flash settings, and composing your shots makes all the difference. Since I'm always so swamped getting things ready before the party, I take my decoration photos the day after the party, cleaning up enough party aftermath, resetting and relighting candles, resetting the fog machine, refilling dry ice, and whatever else needs to be reset. I set up my tripod, and I usually take at least one shot each with no flash at all, then also with the slow-sync flash setting, and sometimes with full flash. In the photography world, this is called "bracketing" your shots, basically covering all your bases. It is hard to see on the small digital camera screen which shot is the clearest and gives the best impression of what it really looked like in person, so I take one of each so I can compare on my computer later when I download them. Since I used the same bracketing technique before I had a digital camera, you can imagine how many rolls of film I used to develop just for Halloween photos!

Now all those tips are of no real use when the party is actually going on, since even with slow-sync flash you get blurs of people moving, and trying to use a tripod during a party spoils the mood. Sometimes I try anyway just in case it comes out okay since it's digital with no film developing cost, but often those don't come out. If there's only a little bit of blur, once you shrink it down to web size it can look okay, so that's a trick to remember. Usually I just stick to capturing party action with full flash and save my effort for the decoration photos the next day. With the walls being the stone effect, at least even with flash those still have decent Halloween atmosphere.

Broadcasting your Bash

Since 2001 I have been webcasting my Halloween parties, several years now with two webcams to show both inside and graveyard. The first webcam was borrowed from a friend since it was an expensive IP Ethernet webcam. I was able to borrow two of the same for awhile from two friends, but recently I invested in a newer wireless model from the same manufacturer that still requires power but not the extra Ethernet cable. The IP cameras have built-in webservers which is why they are still $300 or more each, but they work great. You can also get software that will use your camcorder as a broadcast webcam, but then that
means you can't use the camcorder for filming other live footage during the party. Most of the super-cheap webcams are not designed for continuous broadcast while not being monitored. Since I use two webcams running on the same subnet, it takes a bit of finagling with my router to configure web port forwarding to have both webcams viewable from outside the LAN, and I use a single HTML page to point to the links of each webcam. The single page doesn't go live until the morning of the party so I don't accidentally broadcast something not suitable for viewing! These webcams actually broadcast their images on the webserver built into the webcam itself,

 so there are only certain display settings available. There is also a technical limit that those IP webcams only allow 10 simultaneous viewers. I have some long-distance friends and family who tune in, plus some strangers who email me that they have watched some of the party.

When dealing with low-light and webcams, my inside webcam usually works well with the candles and other lighting. Since the outside webcam is aimed at the graveyard, and I have "artificial moonlight" with some of those clamp lights so people can read the gravestones, I just have to be sure not to aim the webcam straight into a light source, which works pretty well. If it's a decent quality webcam, and you have enough lighting for people not to trip and fall, then it should be fine for the webcam.

What is fun for me is saving an image every minute so I can go back and see what else happened during the party when I didn't see it in person. I've been able to make stop-motion movies using those images since I've set up the webcams to capture a still image to my home machine every minute during the broadcast. Even if the broadcast dies, I still want the image captures for later, so as long as I notice or someone tells me, I will take the time quickly to fix the webcam by plugging the cord back into power if someone trips over the cable or fixing the alignment if someone knocks the aim wonky. Several hours of partying people collapsed into a couple of minutes is always fun to watch later, at least for me!

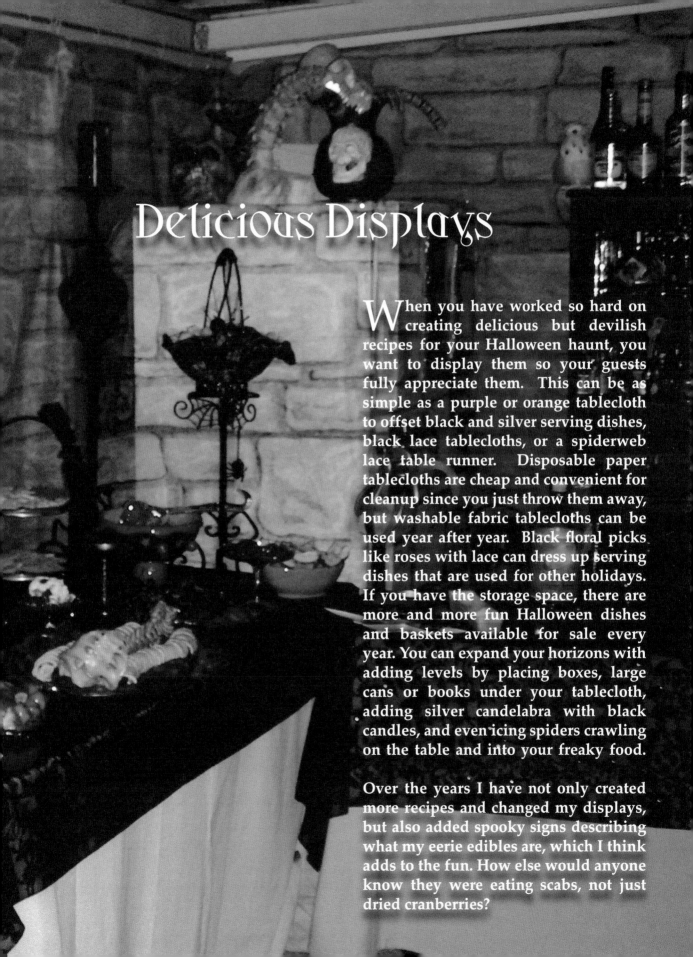

Delicious Displays

When you have worked so hard on creating delicious but devilish recipes for your Halloween haunt, you want to display them so your guests fully appreciate them. This can be as simple as a purple or orange tablecloth to offset black and silver serving dishes, black lace tablecloths, or a spiderweb lace table runner. Disposable paper tablecloths are cheap and convenient for cleanup since you just throw them away, but washable fabric tablecloths can be used year after year. Black floral picks like roses with lace can dress up serving dishes that are used for other holidays. If you have the storage space, there are more and more fun Halloween dishes and baskets available for sale every year. You can expand your horizons with adding levels by placing boxes, large cans or books under your tablecloth, adding silver candelabra with black candles, and even icing spiders crawling on the table and into your freaky food.

Over the years I have not only created more recipes and changed my displays, but also added spooky signs describing what my eerie edibles are, which I think adds to the fun. How else would anyone know they were eating scabs, not just dried cranberries?

I have selected some of my own Delicious Displays so you can see how my arrangements have evolved over the years. By keeping my eyes open at discount stores, over time I have accumulated more party serving dishes like the tiered plate trays that save space and create their own levels instead of arranging boxes under the tablecloth. Some more normal appetizers have been phased out in favor of new theme recipes as I have created them, and I still have needed more room for food! Be sure to have extra space if you are asking guests to bring their own Creepy Cuisine.

Here is Halloween 1999 with the Decayed Corpse Chips with Entrail Salsa upgraded from the original plain chips inside a small cardboard coffin with purple paper napkin lining, to an actual mini skeleton in a larger coffin with velvet lining, plus the first plain paper spooky signs. This shows levels created with boxes and cans underneath a disposable purple paper tablecloth over another matching tablecloth, with a spiderweb lace table runner made from costume scraps and black fringe.

Halloween 2000 used fewer levels underneath the purple paper tablecloth because of even more tiered serving dishes. For variety the purple was the top accent layer over a black paper tablecloth underneath. This was the beginning of the Bizarre Brain, as well as the Sneaky Slices with Golden Goo.

Halloween 2001 I no longer needed levels underneath the tablecloth because I had acquired several more serving dishes and tiered trays, as well as used a gargoyle prop with a crystal platter to elevate the Haunted Human Heart to its traditional place of honor. You can also see the first Freshly Flayed Flesh on Ectoplasm Crusts. That same year I finally improved on the food signs idea by using black cardstock behind printed titles with ripped edges and aged with brown acrylic paint, then glued around black party picks. By carefully washing them and packing them away, these signs have lasted over 5 years!

Halloween 2002 was the debut of Pumpkin Pasties and Butterbeer, repeated by request from that summer's wizard party, and we tried Pumpkin Juice again in the pitcher. The Bizarre Brain became even more unsettling with a bed of leaf lettuce, and that table is almost overflowing with food!

For Halloween 2003 I had moved so was able to have my first graveyard, and I blocked off the front door to send my guests through the graveyard before entering the party. Since I didn't want the food over carpet, I moved it to the front foyer to help block the door, but it was a bit cramped. I decided not to use a purple tablecloth for a change, but still kept the spiderweb lace table runner and the icing spiders crawling around the table. A couple levels reappeared since I used antique wooden cigar boxes that looked nice even though not covered by any tablecloth.

Since I was so low on food table space in 2003, for Halloween 2004 I decided to spread out with some desserts on a separate table than the rest of the freaky food and expand the main table to full length, which barely fit in the foyer.

For Halloween 2005 I decided the front foyer was too confining, so I moved the main food table to the back patio, which gave plenty of room to spread out while still keeping the front door blocked so guests would enter through the graveyard instead. I also inherited a collection of old bottles so I enlarged my Mad Scientist display to incorporate them on my dining room table off the kitchen, including moving most of the edible body parts to the experiment table, freeing up a lot of space on the main food table.

Here is the food table for Halloween 2006 on the screened patio at the first Halloween party held at my house, with plenty of space ready on the black lace tablecloths for guests to bring their own revolting recipes, plus the separate Mad Scientist Body Parts display in the dining area inside.

The Mad Scientist Body Parts and Experiments were inside again for Halloween 2007, and the main food table was full since a separate table was set up for guests to bring their own contributions for the Creepy Cuisine Competition. I provided photo holders and floral picks for cards to hold entry forms to list their recipes and their names so everyone would know who was so clever. The Decayed Corpse Chips were displayed on the glass coffeetable in the living room along with assorted candies and decorations on the spiderweb lace table runner. Can you see the hidden design in the new black lace tablecloths?

Halloween Recipes

Not only are the costumes and decorations fun for Halloween, but I always have to see what creepy, ooky, or just plain visually disgusting party food I can make that still tastes yummy. I think it goes with the spirit of Halloween as a holiday, but not everyone shares my die-hard enthusiasm. Many of my friends can't get past the visuals to find out that what I've made really does taste good, but I can attest that at least most of them give my eerie eats a try. I've been making the yummy gelatin Eerie Eyeballs since 1994, but some of my friends are often too chicken to eat them!

My Halloween Recipes first went online in 1997, and over the years became popular enough among fellow Halloween fans that my page reached the top of Google search results for several years in a row. Here are my favorite recipes, with additional step-by-step photos. Feel free to add your own creative touches when you feel inspired!

Mad Scientist Body Parts

My repertoire of recipes has acquired more and more body parts over the years, and since my Mad Scientist display has also expanded, I have arranged all the edible body parts together as a mad scientist experiment in process, complete with microscopes, notebooks, periodic tables, and lab coat hanging on the wall waiting for the doctor to return. Not only does this enhance the mad scientist theme nicely, but it also frees space on other tables for even more food, especially when guests bring their own disgusting dishes.

The Eerie Eyeballs, Bizarre Brain, Freaky Witches' Fingers and Haunted Human Heart have their own complete recipes listed here. The bleeding hands are made in the same way as the Haunted Human Heart, using peach gelatin with evaporated milk as the flesh, with the same raspberry blood syrup in a plastic baggie bladder inside.
The green substance in the large jar is an assortment of Gummy Body Parts purchased candies suspended in green "ectoplasm" soft-set lime gelatin. Deliciously disgusting!

Mojitoes

I discovered drinking mojitos back in 2002, and since I keep growing mint in my garden, fresh mojitos are a staple for summertime parties with my friends. One Halloween guest was looking at the Mad Scientist Body Parts and started joking about "moji-toes" so of course I took up the challenge!

I first thought of an opaque gelatin shot since it would go with my other gelatin body parts, but the most difficult part was the toe shape. Even though I looked at ice cube trays and candy molds for a longer rounded end shape, I could not find any molds that looked enough like toes, so I made my own using polymer clay originals, washed them thoroughly, then made the molds with food-grade silicone putty now available at craft stores and online. I only made 9 toe molds, so I tailored my recipe to fit that much at once. By mixing up one batch at a time, you can keep enough Mojitoes safe in the fridge for several days until your party.

Mojitoes

Yields approximately 9 large monster toes.

1 envelope plain powdered gelatin
1 1/2 c mojito mixer
1 oz (1/8 cup) light rum (optional)
1/2 c mini marshmallows

Pour 1 1/2 cups mojito mixer into a saucepan over medium low heat. Stir plain powdered gelatin into mojito mixer. After gelatin is dissolved, add 1/2 cup mini marshamallows and keep stirring until marshmallows are completely dissolved. Remove from heat and add 1 oz light rum if desired. Pour into well-oiled toe molds and refrigerate until set. Carefully remove the Mojitoes from the molds, accent the details with food coloring if you like, and serve.

Eerie Eyeballs

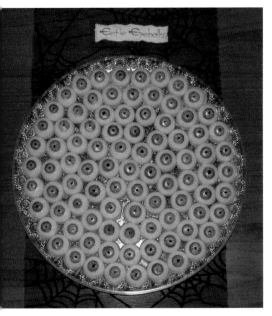

In the early days of my first Halloween parties, I wanted to serve eyeballs that had real squishy eyeball texture instead of the common cocktail onion or deviled egg with green olive iris. My mother had a vintage recipe for a layered gelatin dessert that had a chunky pineapple cream cheese layer, so with experimentation that old recipe was transformed and refined into these Eerie Eyeballs, debuting in 1994. Those brave enough to pick up the squishy eyeball off the plate are rewarded with rich pineapple cheesecake flavor. I used the melonballer technique for years, but it

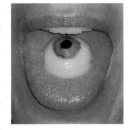

s so much easier to use the truffle candy molds, and at only $2 each mold, you can easily uy enough molds to reuse each year and make your eyeball-making life much easier!

Eerie Eyeballs

Yields approximately 9 dozen bite-sized eyeballs

3 oz (small box) lemon gelatin powdered dessert mix
(can be sugar-free gelatin dessert mix which will be less weight listed on the box label)
1 cup hot water
1/2 cup miniature marshmallows
1 cup pineapple juice
8 oz cream cheese (can be lowfat Neufchatel)

Dissolve lemon gelatin in 1 cup water in double boiler. If you don't have a double boiler, use a netal or glass bowl that fits in aon pan of boiling water. Add marshmallows and stir to melt. e patient and keep stirring since this will take awhile until the marshmallows are completely lissolved. Remove from heat. Add pineapple juice and cream cheese. Beat with a mixer or whisk ntil well blended. Cool slightly. If you have truffle candy molds or round ice cube trays, spray hem with non-stick cooking spray first, then pour the mixture in the molds and leave to set in he refrigerator. Otherwise pour into a deep ceramic lish and chill until thickened and firm enough for cooping into eyeballs. Using a melonballer, scoop ull balls of the mixture and set aside for decoration. f you are using the melonballer method, you might eed to add one package of plain gelatin powder o your mixture. The molds work fine with just he lemon gelatin to make gently squishy eyeballs.

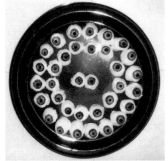

To decorate the eyeballs, use liquid food coloring and an old detail paintbrush and get creative. You will need black food coloring for the pupils. Do not use food coloring pens because they will rip the delicate surface of the gelatin. Start with your iris color, paint the outside circle of the iris, then using as dry a brush as possible, pull the brush from the circle edge inward, getting lighter towards the center, and leaving white space between brushstrokes for the striated effect of a real iris. Paint all the irises, then the first eyeballs will be dry enough to start adding the black pupils. Refrigerate until serving, but remember that the longer your decorated eyeballs sit, the more the coloring will bleed into the gelatin and your detail becomes fuzzy. Wash your brush well and keep it as your food decorating brush. You can paint whatever colors you like for the irises, but I keep mine all the same color to save time, plus I have a good story why. I was asked once why all my eyeballs were blue, so I informed them that after freezing the melanin breaks down so no matter what the original color, all eyeballs become blue. I know this from years of dissecting cow eyes with my teacher mother since all those brown cow eyes became blue, but it was even more shocking to my guests that I even knew that fact!

I did find rubber ice cube trays that worked beautifully with much less waste than the melonballer technique. I sprayed the rubber trays with non-stick cooking spray beforehand like you would any gelatin mold, let the gelatin mixture sit in the refrigerator to set, then I was able to carefully pop the eyeballs out to paint them. Some of the eyeballs did break, and they do have one flat side, but that works well, since then they don't roll around while you are trying to paint them. The ice cube holes were deep enough to be difficult to clean, and I learned the hard way they were not dishwasher safe. Since 2001 I have found that truffle candy molds are even better, since the swirl design on the top is the right size for the cornea shape on the eyeball. When using the truffle molds, one recipe makes about 9 dozen eyeballs, which is plenty for a party crowd!

Freaky Witches Fingers

Over the years many people have developed their own recipes for edible fingers. I found the original Creepy Witches' Fingers recipe long ago on the Searchable Online Archive of Recipes, which has now moved to Recipe Source. The original recipe listed baking powder in the ingredients but baking soda in the instructions. After years of using baking powder just fine, when moving to a different oven, my witches' fingers kept puffing during baking, which was highly disappointing to say the least. I realized that the dough was very similar to a Christmas cookie recipe I had, so I just used neither baking powder nor baking soda and had a more shortbread-like recipe that keeps the detail perfectly, since it has no leavening. I now use my adapted recipe and it works every time.

I have also experimented over the years with different fingernails, whether whole almonds with the skin intact, blanched whole almonds, or almond slices. I like the contrast of the whole almonds with brown skin against the pale finger cookie better than the pale spookiness of the blanched almonds, and I often prefer the almond slices as more diseased fingernail effect, but it depends on how I feel that specific Halloween season. I like the clean disembodied finger look, reserving my bloody gore for the gelatin body parts, but you can use red gel icing for bloody stumps and bleeding nail beds if you like. You may also use food coloring in the dough like a few drops of green if your idea of a wicked witch comes from somewhere over the rainbow.

Freaky Witches Fingers

Yields 5 dozen

1 cup butter, softened
1 cup powdered sugar
1 egg
1 tsp almond extract
1 tsp vanilla
2 2/3 cups flour
1 tsp salt
3/4 cup almonds, whole, blanched or sliced
1 tube red decorator gel (optional, not pictured)

In bowl, beat together butter, sugar, egg, almond extract and vanilla. Beat in flour and salt. Cover and refrigerate at least 30 minutes. Working with one quarter of the dough at a time and keeping remainder refrigerated, roll heaping teaspoonful of dough into finger shape for each cookie. Squeeze twice along finger length to create knuckle shapes. Press almond firmly into one end for nail. After arranging on the lightly greased baking sheets, make slashes with a paring knife across in several places to form knuckles. Clusters of three slashes for each knuckle looks best.

Bake in 325° F (160° C) oven for 20-25 minutes or until pale golden. Let cool for 3 minutes. Lift up almond, squeeze red decorator gel onto nail bed and press almond back in place, so gel oozes out from underneath. You can also make slashes in the finger and fill them with "blood." If you are opting for less gore, you will still need spare icing to glue the almond nails to the cookies after baking, since otherwise they fall off too easily during storage and serving.

When cool enough to stay intact, remove fingers from baking sheets and let cool on racks before storing. Repeat with remaining dough. Baked cookies will keep in an airtight container for at least two weeks. Unbaked mixed dough can be kept refrigerated for at least a week. Arrange for serving attractively on a plate, reaching up out of an urn of chocolate cookie crumb dirt, crawling out of a basket, or your own creative idea.

Brittle Bones

Bone cookies are also not unusual, but I wanted a crispy bonelike texture for my cookies, so meringue's the thing and naturally bakes to a nice bone color without additional decorating. One day I may attempt a meringue skeleton, but it is easier to get into a rhythm of piping the same bone shape to yield as much as 14 dozen. These

are fragile, so some will break when removing them from the parchment paper, and they absorb moisture in the air and get gooey, so bring these out only immediately before guests arrive and don't set them near a fog machine, punch bowl or other sources of moisture if possible.

Brittle Bones

Yields approximately 14 dozen small finger bones

3 large egg whites
1/4 tsp cream of tartar
1/8 tsp salt
2/3 cup white sugar
1/2 tsp vanilla

Preheat oven to 200° F. Line cookie sheet with brown paper bag or parchment. In a medium sized bowl at high speed, beat egg whites, cream of tartar and salt till fluffy. Gradually beat in sugar. Add vanilla. Place in pastry bag fitted with a medium plain piping tip. Pipe 3" bone shapes onto parchment or brown paper bag. Bake 1 hour until set. Turn off oven, dry in oven 1 hour. Be sure to store in completely airtight reusable plastic food containers or they will become soggy from moisture in the air

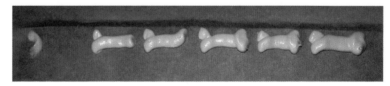

Bizarre Brain Pate

One year in July a friend gave me a brain mold for my birthday, obviously knowing my love of Halloween, so I used a recipe I had found for Mardi Gras and adapted it for my brain mold. I could have used a sweet gelatin recipe like other body parts, but I thought menu balance with a savory addition was a better choice. The shrimp gives a nice pale pink smooth brain texture, and I use my fine paintbrush with some watery gray food coloring to accent and shade the brain folds. The leftovers make great sandwiches!

Bizarre Brain Pate

half a can cream of mushroom soup
(full can is 10 3/4 oz)
4 ounces cream cheese, softened
(can be lowfat Neufchatel)
1 (1/4 oz) envelope powdered unflavored gelatin,
softened in 1/4 cup water
1 pounds frozen cooked shrimp, finely chopped
(or 1 pound crab meat)
1/2 cup mayonnaise
1 Tbsp lemon juice
Tabasco or creole seasoning to taste

Pour the powdered unflavored gelatin into 1/4 cup water and let stand to bloom. Chop the frozen shrimp finely in a food processor or blender, until almost a paste. This is easier when the shrimp is still frozen hard. Heat undiluted soup and mix in the half-block of cream cheese. Remove the mushrooms or blend the soup before adding to the mixture if you are concerned they will show in your brain texture. Stir in softened gelatin and blend well. Fold in remaining ingredients and pour into a lightly-oiled mold. Chill until firm and serve with your favorite crackers

Freshly Flayed Flesh on Ectoplasm Crusts

I was looking for more savory options for my maniacal menu, so I remembered the ever-popular smoked salmon with cream cheese and came up with these. Be sure to use the vivid pink oil-packed smoked salmon to really look like freshly flayed flesh!

Freshly Flayed Flesh on Ectoplasm Crusts

Yields about 3 dozen bite-sized appetizers

1 package oil-packed sliced smoked salmon
1 package cream cheese (can be lowfat Neufchatel)
1 package crackers, melba toasts, bagel chips, or be creative!

Cut the smoked salmon into small thin strips. Spread a dollop of cream cheese on each cracker, then place a strip of smoked salmon curled on top of the cream cheese. This is another standard tasty appetizer just renamed to be gory for the season!

Sinister Skulls

I found little plastic skull candy cups at a party store, but it took awhile before I thought of how to use them. You can mold cream cheese into any container for any holiday, but white skulls with bloody sauce goes so nicely for Halloween.

Sinister Skulls

plastic wrap
1 small plastic skull candy container
1 block of cream cheese
(can be lowfat Neufchatel)
1 jar chili sauce or salsa
crackers

Set the block of cream cheese out to thaw to room temperature. Line the inside of the plastic skull dish with plastic wrap leaving enough edges to wrap around later. Spoon the softened cream cheese into the plastic-lined skull dish, mashing in as much cream cheese as possible to pick up the most detail in the mold. Scrape any extra cream cheese off the top so it is flat. Close the plastic wrap over the flat cream cheese top and place in the freezer to set. Once set, remove the plastic wrap from the skull dish, and carefully wrap in foil to cushion the face shape. Line the skull dish with fresh plastic wrap to make more cream cheese skulls. Store in the freezer until night before the party, then thaw in the refrigerator. To serve, place the skull in a shallow dish, garnish with your preferred bloody salsa or chili mixture, including inside the eye sockets, and stab with your favorite spreader. You can extend the time before needing to refill by placing the skull on half a block of cream cheese, but cover the plain cream cheese with enough sauce so you can only see the skull above the "blood."

Fried Spiders

Inspired by the traditional Cambodian delicacy, in 2003 I tried making my own Fried Spiders out of pre-made ingredients. They are quite fragile, but tasty!

For each fried spider:
1 frozen breaded cream-cheese-filled jalapeño popper
4 frozen ready-to-bake breaded onion rings
egg wash
wooden toothpicks soaked in water

Soak the wooden toothpicks for at least 30 minutes. Thaw the ready-to-bake jalapeño poppers and onion rings enough to be able to use toothpicks and knives on them. Cut the onion rings in half to make the curved legs. Attach the 8 legs to the jalapeño pepper body with egg wash and hold in place with the wet toothpicks. Bake in the oven according to the jalapeño popper package instructions, taking care not to burn the legs. Carefully arrange on a serving platter, since the legs might fall off, just like real fried spiders!

Decayed Corpse Chips with Entrail Salsa

As you can tell, often a very normal dish can be turned nasty just by giving it a disgustingly clever name. Think up your own names for your favorite appetizers to give them a Halloween spin.

Decayed Corpse Chips with Entrail Salsa

blue corn tortilla chips
coffin
salsa

This isn't so much a recipe as it is a creative display. Arrange the blue corn chips in a napkin-lined coffin in the shape of a long-dead corpse. The natural blue corn chips have almost a dusky shade of brown in them that hints of decayed skin. Serve with a nice blood-red chunky salsa as accompanying entrails.

When I found a larger coffin that happened to fit a rubber skeleton I had for years, I lined the coffin with crushed velvet, propped up the skeleton inside so he wasn't completely buried in chips, arranged the chips around him, and set the crystal bowl of "entrails" between his calves. If you cannot find a coffin, find a clean plastic skull or assorted bones, put them in a large serving bowl, then arrange the blue chips around the bones as the decaying flesh.

Batato Chips

2 lbs purple potatoes, cut into
1/8-inch thick slices
3 Tbsp olive oil
coarse salt
(cayenne pepper to taste)
(ground pepper to taste)

Preheat oven to 400° F. Thinly slice purple potatoes on a mandolin slicer or cut carefully with a sharp knife. Use a metal cookie cutter to cut bat shapes out of the potato slices. A plastic cookie cutter will not be strong enough to cut through the raw potato. Lightly coat 2 rimmed baking sheets with cooking spray, set aside. Put potatoes, oil, 1 Tbsp salt (and cayenne if desired) in a large bowl, and season with pepper

to taste. Toss to combine and completely coat the potatoes with oil. Place slices on prepared baking sheets at least 1/4-inch apart. Bake at 400° F for 7 minutes, then rotate the baking sheets and bake another 7 minutes. Chips should be crispy and curling slightly at the edges. Sprinkle with salt immediately while the chips are still on the baking sheets, then turn chips over onto parchment paper or paper towels to absorb excess oil. Use the leftover salt on the baking

sheets to salt the other side of the chips, then let them cool and dry completely before serving.

Look for purple potatoes at gourmet grocery stores or farmers markets. If you cannot find purple potatoes, you can use russett potatoes for albino bats or try soaking your potato slices in water tinted with food coloring of your choice, but your guests tongues will end up matching the food coloring. You can save your potato slice scraps and bake them with your chips, since they're tasty snacks as you're preparing for your party!

Savory Spiders with Gooey Guts

Yields 5 spiders.

1 package pop-open plain buttermilk biscuits
(not extra flaky, not cinnamon rolls)

Vegetarian Gooey Guts
nacho cheese sauce of your choice

Carnivore Gooey Guts
your favorite crumbled pre-cooked sausage
mixed with cheese sauce
or use your favorite sausage roll filling recipe

Preheat oven to 400° F per the package instructions. Use an ungreased non-stick baking sheet. Each spider requires two pre-shaped biscuits. Using clean kitchen shears, cut about 1/3rd of one

biscuit away to be the head, then cut the remaining 2/3rds into 4 skinny strips for the legs. Twist the both ends of each strip to be pointy spider feet. Form the shortest strip it into a curved U-shape to be the back legs. Making sure they all touch, use the two the longer strips for the middle legs, then the other smaller strip curved into another U-shape for the front legs. All the legs should be touching each other in the middle underneath where the body will go. Take the other whole biscuit and tuck all the edges in to make a smooth ball. Place the tucked edges side down making firm contact on top the legs. Take the 1/3rd biscuit,

tuck the edges in for a smooth ball for the head, then place the head in front touching the body.

If you want your spiders to have Gooey Guts, you can add the guts inside the body and head when you are tucking in the edges before assembling the spider. Put the cheese sauce into a baggie and cut one corner to make a piping hole. Shape the whole biscuit so it is curved and almost closed into a ball, then pipe the cheese sauce into the biscuit and seal the last edges around the cheese. Place the biscuit seam side down onto the legs. Usually the head is too small to fit cheese inside without making a giant mess, but you are welcome to try!

Bake the spider biscuits no more than 6 minutes at 400° F or the legs will burn. Your spiders will be barely golden brown but tasty, fluffy and tender.

Spooky Sugar Cookies

Rolled cookies with cookie cutters are a staple for all holidays, and can become ghosts, pumpkins, black cats, gargoyles or gravestones just by finding the right cutter shape. This sugar cookie recipe from my aunt has proven itself over the years as failsafe, as well as being only sweet enough so that their flavor supports sweet icing nicely. These are easily made non-dairy by using non-dairy margarine and water instead of butter and milk.

Spooky Sugar Cookies

Yields 5 or 6 dozen standard cookie cutter shapes

2 cups margarine or butter
2 1/4 cups sugar
3 eggs
1 1/2 tsp vanilla
6 cups flour
3/4 tsp salt
4 Tbsp milk (can use water)

Cream sugar into softened butter. Add eggs then remaining ingredients. Only add milk or water if the dough is too dry. Chill 1 hour. Unbaked mixed dough can be refrigerated for at least one week before baking. Roll out one-sixth of dough 1/8 to 1/4 inch thick and cut with cookie cutter of your choice. Place on a greased cookie sheet and bake at 375° F (190° C) for 12 minutes. If making different shapes, group similar size shapes on the same sheets for even baking. These can be frosted. After icing is completely dry, these can be stored in an airtight container for at least two weeks or longer.

Buttercream Frosting

Thanks to Kathy Henricks for her tried & true frosting recipe! This frosting is perfect for icing cakes and hand-spreading onto cookies since it stays soft.

1 1/4 cup Crisco shortening (only use Crisco)
2 lbs powdered sugar
1 tsp salt
1/2 cup water
2 Tbsp light corn syrup
1 tsp butter flavoring
1 tsp vanilla

Beat 5 to 10 minutes with a power mixer until very smooth. Water down a small amount for a crumb coat if frosting a cake. After 20 minutes (when set), frost with remainder of frosting. When set, use paper towel or typing paper to set desired surface texture. This is fluffy enough to spread easily with a knife onto cakes or cookies, yet stiff enough for keeping its shape for piping and decorating.

Ghoulish Gravestones

For the Ghoulish Gravestone cookies, use the Spooky Sugar Cookies recipe with a gravestone cookie cutter, bake and cool completely, then cover with Royal Icing. The buttercream frosting is too soft for these cookies since you cannot write on the surface of the frosting. Tint the icing gray using a small amount of black food coloring, then add just enough light corn syrup for the icing to level itself when spread, but so it still hardens enough to use food coloring pens for the lettering. Be sure to wait a full day or at least overnight for the royal icing to harden completely before using the food coloring pens. Food coloring pen sets have become available in most large grocery stores with the cake decorating supplies, plus specialty cake decorating stores or online. If you cannot find any, use a fine, soft watercolor brush and normal black food coloring.

You can use any lettering style you like for your gravestone epitaphs, and you can vary your font styles as you wish. If you are overwhelmed by the concept of free-hand lettering, print out your epitaphs from your computer in fonts you like and the layout centered to your preference, then use those as models to draw on the cookies. I say "draw" because elaborate lettering by hand is much more like drawing than writing, since you are placing each line for the end result image, not just writing quickly to get words down.

I hadn't made gravestone cookies in the past since the only cookie cutters I found were the simple upside-down U shape, which I thought too boring, but I found a more elaborate cutter the same year I made my first outside gravestone decorations, so I thought the theme very appropriate! My first year I wanted to be sure the epitaphs were legible so everyone would get the jokes, which they did, and I was going for a simple carved style. The next year I kicked myself because I've been good at free-hand calligraphy since I was 9 years old, so why not go all out with the lettering? I chose a consistent Old English blackletter font style since I liked the look and can do it in my sleep since I've done it free-hand so many years now. Since I hadn't used the "punny" epitaphs for my yard gravestones, I used them on my cookies, using the same 13 epitaphs that made me laugh the most for the entire batch of cookies. The only drawback to making these cookies every year is that in only 4 years my black food coloring pen has already run out of ink!

Royal Icing

This is the traditional recipe that glues gingerbread houses together or makes a hard candy-like surface on cookies or cakes. Use this recipe for the Awful Arachnids and the Ghoulish Gravestones. If you are making spiders and icing cookies with Royal Icing, make one large batch, tint gray, reserve about 1 cup in another bowl for your spiders and tightly cover. Thin the rest of the icing with corn syrup for smoothly-iced cookies, then you still have your stiff Royal Icing ready to be tinted black for spiders!

Royal Icing

Makes enough to ice 5-6 dozen sugar cookies

16 oz powdered sugar
3 egg whites
1/2 tsp cream of tartar

Beat until peaks firmly hold their shape, the more you beat it, the firmer the frosting. This hardens when exposed to air, but dissolves in water, so keep a moist towel over the bowl while working with it. Use a tight-fitting plastic container to store in the refrigerator for a couple weeks, but the egg whites begin to separate from the sugar any longer than that. Hard royal icing decorations like spiders can last indefinitely if kept away from moisture. If you are concerned about using raw egg whites, you can purchase pasteurized eggs, or you can use

meringue powder found at specialty baking stores.

Awful Arachnids

These edible spiders are made from Royal Icing, which needs to be used right away since it hardens to a rocklike texture very quickly! Mix up the Royal Icing per the recipe, and add black gel food coloring to get the mixture as dark as you can. It will dry a darker color than your wet icing looks. I only made a third of the Royal Icing recipe and I still had a lot of icing left over after making two dozen spiders.

These are very fragile, especially when peeling them off the waxed paper, since the legs tend to break off. Place gently around your party table for a spooky look, but if you place near moisture, you might have a black food coloring mess that will be difficult to clean! I used a decorating cone with plain round writing tip to pipe the icing into spider shapes on waxed paper.

At the left and right are finished spiders, then left to right shows what I pipe on a sheet of waxed paper. I pipe the legs first, then plop on a small

round blob for the head, then I make sure the outside edge of the body touches all the legs, then fill it in with a bigger blob for the body to stand up higher than the head or legs.

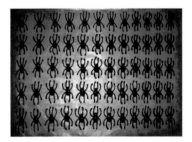

If your hand gets sore from piping spiders like mine does, put a toothpick in the piping tube nozzle so the icing doesn't dry and plug the nozzle. Taking breaks is good since the warmer the icing gets, the bigger and sloppier your lines become, so let the icing bag rest back to room temperature, then keep piping away until you get sick of spiders! For me that's usually about 3 dozen, or one cookie sheet full, and usually happens over the course of several days while watching TV and waiting for other Halloween recipes to set or bake. Once the spiders are dry, as long as they stay away from moisture, they will keep indefinitely.

Pumpkin Pasties

Inspired by a popular children's book series and now one of the most popular items on my Halloween menu, these tasty treats put traditional pumpkin pie into bite-sized packages as perfect appetizers.

Pumpkin Pasties

Yields about 3 dozen miniature pasties

2 eggs, slightly beaten
3/4 cup sugar
1 lb can pumpkin
(or 2 cups fresh, roasted in the oven then strained)
1/2 tsp salt
1 tsp cinnamon
1/2 tsp ginger
1/4 tsp cloves
1 2/3 cups evaporated milk (1 can)
1/2 tsp allspice
9 oz pie crust pastry (enough for two single standard pie crusts)

Bake the pie filling only (no crust) in a large greased casserole dish in hot oven (425° F) for 15 minutes. Keep oven door closed and reduce temp to moderate (350° F) and continue baking for 45 minutes or until table knife inserted in center of dish comes out clean. Cool on wire rack.

Make or purchase pie crust pastry. Roll thin and cut into circles approximately 4" in diameter. Put a spoonful of the cooled pumpkin mixture towards one side of the center of the circle. Fold

over the crust into a half-circle and firmly crimp the edges closed. Place on a greased cookie sheet, slice three small slits in the top for venting, and bake only until crust is a light golden-brown. The pumpkin filling will begin to make the crust soggy when stored over time, so these are best baked the day of serving. These can be made ahead by freezing the assembled pasties unbaked on cookie sheets, then thawed and baked the day of serving. Great served at room-temperature, then you don't have to worry about your guests possibly burning their mouths from the steaming hot pumpkin inside!

Spicy Bat Wings

This is another creative description of a familiar dish. Since I am not one for extremely spicy food, I used honey barbecue wings, but you can use spicy buffalo wings or your own spicy chicken wing recipe. Bats are a more obvious choice for Halloween, but these could be Gargoyle Wings or Raven Wings as well!

Bake purchased chicken wings according to the package instructions. Arrange and serve, making sure you have a sign to identify them as something spooky instead of just chicken!

Sneaky Slices with Golden Goo

Vivid blood-red apple skins against the snow-white apple flesh look fabulous on a Halloween table, with the caramel "golden goo" ready in a bowl for dipping.

Sneaky Slices with Golden Goo

sliced apples
purchased caramel dipping sauce
(not ice cream topping)

A spin on a traditional Halloween treat of caramel apples without all the mess! Cut the apples into slices if not already. Pre-sliced apples can be purchased now in snack-size bags, which are not only a time-saver, but they have been treated with citric acid so will not turn brown.

Dried Scabs

Yes, another nasty name for an otherwise mediocre dried fruit, but call them "scabs" and all of a sudden no one will eat them!

Arrange the dried cranberries in a bowl or dish. Be sure you have a sign to identify them as something spooky. You can use any small flat dried fruit like currants, cherries, or even blueberries, but raisins are usually too plump to be scabs.

Tooth Decay Fodder

This is my attempt to make even one of the best parts of Halloween scary by naming it with the possible consequences of overindulgence.

Arrange your favorite Halloween candy in a bowl or coffin. I prefer classic candy corn in a large skull bowl.

Shapely Sandwiches

sliced bread of your choice
sandwich filling of your choice
condiments of your choice
Halloween cookie cutters

Make your sandwiches however you'd like, but try to have ingredients that will stick together and not fall apart after the sandwiches have been cut. The metal cookie cutters work best, since not all the plastic ones are as tall to cut through all the bread and fillings. I used turkey and cheddar cheese, ham and swiss cheese with just a little mayonnaise to moisten the bread, and herbed cheese spreads for my variety of sandwiches. I used a pumpkin cookie cutter for the ones shown.

Spiderweb Brie En Croute

Wrap a packaged puff pastry sheet around a small round of Brie cheese, sealing the raw edges together underneath. Use the leftover pastry scraps to add your own design to the top of the Brie, gluing on the pastry with water, milk or egg wash. Cookie cutters might give you inspiration, or roll your scraps into thin ropes and make a spiderweb design. Brush with milk or egg wash for nice browning. Place on greased foil on a cookie sheet and bake in the oven at 400° F for 15 minutes, or until crust is golden brown. Serve with a spreader and your preferred assortment of crackers.

You can leave your Brie en Croute plain which is still tasty, or you can add a layer between the pastry and the Brie if you like. My favorites are my homemade spiced loquat jam, or apricot preserves with dried cranberries. Any large chunks of fruit make the pastry surface lumpy, so that could mar your design if your work is intricate.

Creepy Cheese and Crackers

For 1999, I used a cookie stamp on melted American cheese while it was cooling in a flat cookie sheet. After it cooled thoroughly, I trimmed away the edges and had what you see at right. For 2006 I finally had time to use my mini Halloween cookie cutters to cut the cheese shapes into white ghosts, orange pumpkins and white skulls.

Tricky Crab Triangles

one stick (1/2 cup) melted butter
one 6 1/2 oz can crab meat
1 small jar (approximately 5 oz) Kraft Old English cheese
1/2 cup mayonnaise
1/2 tsp. garlic salt
one package split English muffins

Combine first 5 ingredients, spread on muffins, put on cookie sheet and freeze. When frozen, cut each muffin into eight triangles. Put in plastic bag, return to freezer. When ready to use, put under broiler until bubbly. As you can see, these really aren't so tricky!

Original Butterbeer

This Butterbeer recipe was originally created for a wizard party, now appearing annually for Halloween by popular demand!

Makes 2 quarts.

1 cup butterscotch schnapps
7 cups cream soda (almost one 2 liter bottle)

Carefully mix just before serving, adding the schnapps to the soda then stirring gently to mix well, or the fizz will dissipate too soon. To keep butterbeer on hand, pour 1 cup cream soda out of the 2-liter bottle, quickly add 1 cup butterscotch schnapps, and recap the bottle. There is not much alcohol content in the butterbeer mixture, just enough to make a small elf tipsy and to give it the warm, buttery aftertaste to the fizzy cream soda.

Butterbeer Light

I improved on the well-loved Original Butterbeer recipe -- now all the alcohol and calories have been charmed away!

Makes 2 quarts.

1 cup sugar-free butterscotch
or English Toffee flavoring syrup
7 cups diet cream soda (almost one 2 liter bottle)

Carefully mix just before serving, adding the butterscotch flavoring to the soda then stirring gently to mix well, or the fizz will dissipate too soon. To keep butterbeer on hand, pour 1 cup cream soda out of the 2-liter bottle, quickly add 1 cup butterscotch flavoring, and recap the bottle. Completely sugar-free and alcohol-free!

Witches' Brew

This recipe fills a 12-quart cauldron.

four 48 oz cans pineapple juice
one 96 oz bottle orange juice
four 2 liter bottles lemon-lime soda
one 1.75 liter bottle vodka
one 1.75 liter bottle rum

All measurements are approximate. Adjust to your own taste. Mix well. Pour into your cauldron, preferably with chunks of dry ice to create the bubbling steam effect. Be careful NOT to drink or eat or in any way come in direct contact with skin with any chunks of dry ice - you can get burned by the extreme cold!

Reanimate Your Own Zombie

This is a mad scientist experiment individual serving alcoholic cocktail in a small glass.

hydrochloric acid = light rum
perchloric acid = spiced rum
tincture of iodine = dark rum
sulfuric acid = Bacardi 151
citric acid = pineapple juice

"To Reanimate Zombies: Into a small beaker, pour equal parts hydrochloric acid, perchloric acid, tincture of iodine & sulfuric acid. Add a splash of citric acid, stir and feed to your corpse for instant reanimation."

Spontaneous Sentience

This is a mad scientist experiment individual serving alcoholic cocktail in a small glass.

benzene = peach schnapps
lactic acid compound = caramel cream liqueur
(can substitute Irish Cream liqueur or similar)
life blood extract = raspberry syrup

"Spontaneous Sentience: Pour benzene into a small beaker. Slowly add lactic acid compound as your brain tissue appears, then carefully add the life blood extract to the brain tissue."

Haunted Human Heart

It probably surprises no one that I have been a fan of Penn & Teller's brand of dark humor for years, so I had not only seen them in person including getting autographs, but also read their book "How to Play With Your Food" (© 1992 by Buggs & Rudy Discount Corp.), so had seen their Bleeding Heart recipe and wanted to try it someday. I finally had my chance when I found a plastic human heart mold more than a decade ago at a specialty gift store around Halloween season. The mold came with a very similar recipe to make the gelatin opaque, but not any instructions to make it bleed, so I adapted Penn & Teller's recipe to create my own, and it has been one of my Halloween favorites ever since. You can find human heart molds online as well as at local Halloween stores. Penn & Teller used a Valentine's Day-style heart-shaped cake pan, but for Halloween I think using the human heart mold improves on their concept one-hundred percent!

I display my heart onto a crystal pedestal plate, then use food coloring and a small brush to accent the veins. I even use red food coloring to shade the muscle contours, since it really does make a difference. One year I had a cardiology intern attend my party, and she said my gelatin heart looked very realistic. Needless to say I was very proud at such high praise! I use my large Psycho-style butcher knife to sever and serve my Haunted Human Heart.

Haunted Human Heart

For the heart:	For the blood:
1 large 6 oz box raspberry gelatin dessert	1/2 cup light corn syrup
small 5 oz can of unsweetened evaporated milk	1/2 cup raspberry syrup drink flavoring
(can use fat-free)	1 Tbsp raspberry liqueur (optional)
1 packet unflavored powdered gelatin	1 drop blue food coloring
1 cup boiling water	1 thin plastic non-zip sandwich bag

Thoroughly wash your mold, especially all the detail where the veins are. When completely dry, spray the mold with non-stick cooking spray. Use a larger bowl or crumpled foil around the outside to support your mold so the top surface will be level. Put the flavored gelatin in a large bowl and stir in 1 cup of boiling water. Stir about 3 minutes until completely dissolved. When slightly cooled, stir in the evaporated milk for one minute, otherwise the milk might curdle. Pour half of the mixture into the heart mold and refrigerate until it is soft-set, as the box instructions recommend for adding fresh fruit.

While the mold is setting, mix the corn syrup and raspberry syrup, plus raspberry liqueur if you like, with one drop of blue food coloring for a nice deep red blood color. Pour your blood into one corner of the thin plastic bag, squeeze the bag carefully to prevent air bubbles, then tie a knot so that the bladder will fit completely inside the rest of the mold, with enough space so gelatin will completely surround the bag. Trim the extra plastic off at the knot. Once the gelatin is soft-set and will support the bag of blood but without a skin on top of the gelatin, arrange the bag of blood, pour the remaining gelatin mixture up to the top of the mold, then refrigerate overnight. If you wait too long to add the remaining gelatin, the layers will not meld together, then your illusion is ruined when the top slides off the bottom, revealing your secret bag of blood!

Once the gelatin is completely set, gently remove the heart from the mold and place on a serving plate, then use food coloring and a small soft watercolor brush to accent the veins. Use red food coloring to shade the contours of the muscle tissue, and blue food coloring to accent the veins. As you can see in the photo above, an unpainted heart is still alarming, but the accents make it so much more realistic. Refrigerate until the party, then display proudly, clarifying to all your guests that "Yes, that is our dessert!"

When ready to sever and serve, call all your guests to come watch the Haunted Human Heart. Enlist a volunteer to hold a glass or bowl to catch the spilling blood. Using a large knife, the scarier the better, stab directly down into the heart, making sure you poke the point of the knife into the plastic bag of blood. Twist the knife to widen the hole in the bag, then guide the knife down to cut a slice through the edge of the heart. Widen the opening in the heart so blood begins to flow. Gently tilt the plate so the blood can easily flow into the cup in your volunteer's hand as your guests all groan in disgust. If anyone actually wants to eat a slice, be careful not to serve any chunks of the plastic bag, and be sure to drizzle extra blood on each slice. If you have willing bodies, feel lucky, since I often have no one willing to eat any of my heart except me!

Parting Words

You have now absorbed a huge helping of Halloween how-tos! Once you digest them all, I hope that you are inspired to adapt these ideas to host your own haunted happenings. Eventually you might find yourself so deep in party plans that the stress starts overtaking the joy of creativity, so stop, sit back, take a deep breath, and remember this: No matter how basic or elaborate you decide to be, above all please always remember that the whole point is to have fun!

Happy Haunting!

Eerie Elegance Extras

Sample Party To-Do List

Week Before Party

bake gravestone cookies
royal icing on gravestone cookies
draw lettering on gravestone cookies (royal icing must set at least 8 hours first)
mix up royal icing for spiders & start piping spiders
bake meringue bones
prep pumpkin pasties on baking sheets & freeze unbaked
bake witches fingers
set out black candles & flesh candles
design & print quizzes
cut quiz sheets
finish costume if not already done!

Two Days Before Party

shop for fresh groceries, plus anything else needed for recipes not already purchased
oil all molds for heart, hands & eyeballs
clear space in fridge for gelatin body parts
cut & bake Batato Chips - keep in large airtight container after cooling
make human heart (decorate next day)
make bleeding hands (decorate next day)
make eyeballs (decorate next day)
make brain pate (decorate next day)
make Mojitoes (not many molds so will need to repeat several times)
pipe more icing spiders
thaw Party Swirls in fridge
thaw cream cheese skulls in fridge
make more Mojitoes
decorate as much as possible

One Day Before Party

vacuum
make more Mojitoes
make eyeballs
make more Mojitoes
run outside webcam cable through back window
run webcam power cord
aim & focus webcam
cut Creepy Cheese slices with mini cookie cutters ghosts, skulls, pumpkins
arrange Creepy Cheese slices on plate, cover & refrigerate
make more Mojitoes
decorate human heart
decorate brain pate
decorate hands
more Mojitoes
set up brie in pastry & refrigerate

set out decorations
cut up new lace tablecloths and arrange on tables
decorate patio as portrait gallery

decorate eyeballs
decorate Mojitoes
green gelatin in large jar for gummy body parts - needs to set for adding fruit per in-structions
clean kitchen floor after gelatin & flour
shower & sleep!

Day of Party

set up webcams for live broadcast
check image capture from webcams
clean bathrooms
clean all mirrors
clean house where needed

10am get dry ice, regular ice, any last groceries
set up candy in skull bowl
cut, form & bake Savory Spiders
bake pumpkin pasties - prepped on baking sheets in freezer
arrange all serving dishes on tables ready for food
prep mad scientist display on kitchen table after kitchen table clear from food prep
set out luminaria jars with tealight candles around backyard
prune dusty miller for Ghostly Greenery
hang ghosts in trees in backyard

hang large web on back wall
set up gravestones in front & back
set up pirate corner

cut & arrange "flayed flesh" on tray & refrigerate covered
cut celery sticks
arrange veggies - celery sticks, mini peppers, broccoli, baby carrots
make 6 qts sugar-free lemonade & refrigerate
pour potions into mad scientist display per labels
cut kiwi into eyeball slices
cut pears into wedges with skin on
cut plums into wedges
cut grapes into small bunches with scissors

set out dried cranberry scabs
arrange blue chips & salsa in coffin
arrange baked pumpkin pasties
arrange witches fingers
arrange gravestone cookies
arrange crackers
set out icing spiders

cut & arrange fruit
cut & arrange apple slices with caramel dip
set out cream cheese skulls & chili sauce
set out brain pate
set out heart mold
set out Mojitoes
set out hands
set up meringue bones very last (get soggy in moist air)

6:00 put on costume
6:15 bake pastry brie to cool before serving
start fog machines on timers
turn on all outside lighting
light candles outside & inside

6:45 pour lemonade in cauldron & add dry ice into infuser ball
add dry ice to mad scientist display
set out "flayed flesh" only when people start arriving
take out eyeballs from fridge
have crab puffs set up on tray in freezer to put in oven later

7pm party begins - have fun! :)

~*~ Spooky Scramble ~*~

Unscramble the authors' names for these chilling classics.

1. The Picture of Dorian Gray
RADEL OWISC

2. Fall of the House of Usher
PEDGE NELLA OAR

3. Frankenstein or the Modern Prometheus
YELLOW FRACTAL LOST YERN MESH

4. Dracula
TOMB RAKERS

5. Dr. Jekyll & Mr. Hyde
TONNE VESTS BRIOUL ROSE

6. The Phantom of the Opera
LOXAN GROUSTE

7. The Legend of Sleepy Hollow
WAITING GRON SHIVN

8. The Haunting of Hill House
SHORES JILYNACK

9. Interview with the Vampire
RENE ICAN

10. The Call of Cthulhu
VELCRO PHAFT

11. Carrie
GESTEN PHINK

12. Harry Potter and the Goblet of Fire
GROW J LINK

13. Cruel Tricks for Dear Friends
LIPNELL JEN DATE TRENTEL

~*~ Name .... ~*~

Spooky Scramble Answers: 1. Oscar Wilde 2. Edgar Allen Poe 3. Mary Wollstonecraft Shelley 4. Bram Stoker 5. Robert Louis Stevenson 6. Gaston Leroux 7. Washington Irving 8. Shirley Jackson 9. Anne Rice 10. H.P. Lovecraft 11. Stephen King 12. J.K. Rowling 13. Penn Jillette and Teller

Genuine Gravestones Answers: 1. H 2. F 3. A 4. I 5. C 6. B 7. D 8. M 9. E 10. L 11. G 12. J 13. K